*Critical Guides to French Texts*

17 Marivaux: La Vie de Marianne *and* Le Paysan Parvenu

*Critical Guides to French Texts*

*EDITED BY ROGER LITTLE, WOLFGANG VAN EMDEN, DAVID WILLIAMS*

# MARIVAUX

# La Vie de Marianne *and* Le Paysan parvenu

David Coward

Senior Lecturer in French
University of Leeds

Grant & Cutler Ltd
1982

© Grant & Cutler Ltd
1982
ISBN 0 7293 0141 9

I.S.B.N. 84-499-6036-3

DEPÓSITO LEGAL: V. 2.709 - 1982

Printed in Spain by
Artes Gráficas Soler, S.A., Valencia
for
GRANT & CUTLER LTD
11 BUCKINGHAM STREET, LONDON, W.C.2.

# CONTENTS

## Prefatory note

References throughout are to the text of *La Vie de Marianne* and *Le Paysan parvenu*, edited by Michel Gilot, in the Garnier-Flammarion series. The best editions, however, remain those prepared by Frédéric Deloffre and readers are strongly recommended to consult his substantial introductions, notes, glossaries and selections of contemporary critical reactions. Italicised numbers in parentheses, followed by page references, refer to numbered items in the Bibliography at the end of this volume, in which all editions are fully described.

## *Biographical note*

Pierre Carlet was born in Paris in 1688. When he was ten, his family moved to Riom where his father was later to become 'directeur des monnaies'. Little is known of his early life. In 1710, he enrolled as a law student in Paris but did not settle in the capital until 1712. Abandoning his studies for writing, he quickly attracted the attention of well-established literary and intellectual figures like Fontenelle and Houdar de La Motte, who introduced him into the *salon* of Mme de Lambert. He was to remain a devotee of *salon* life and after the death of Mme de Lambert in 1733, he transferred his loyalties first to Mme de Tencin and later to Mme Geoffrin. His first published works were novels which attracted little attention, though his comic verse epic, *L'Iliade travestie* (1716) – in which the name Marivaux first appeared – led him to be ranked with the new 'Modernist' movement. He married in 1717 but was left with one daughter when his wife died in 1723 or 1724. Ruined by his investment in Law's Louisiana Bubble in 1720, he applied unsuccessfully for the post at Riom left vacant by his father's death and then resumed his legal studies which he never completed. He turned first to journalism and then to the theatre and gradually acquired a reputation as a subtle but, to some tastes, over-punctilious analyst of human nature. In addition to his numerous early writings, he published three journals, over thirty comedies and his two major unfinished novels. In 1743, he was elected to the French Academy and thereafter wrote little, having both lost his creative impulse and outgrown his public. He died in 1763.

# 1 *Marivaux and the novel*

The first book of *La Vie de Marianne* appeared in 1731 and its eleventh part was published in 1742. Between these dates, Marivaux also wrote thirteen of his thirty-four comedies, the eleven issues of *Le Cabinet du Philosophe* (1734) and the five parts of *Le Paysan parvenu* (1734-5). His output at this time was as varied as it was prodigious. Not only did he emerge with an enhanced reputation as essayist, playwright and novelist, but his two novels seem to have been written in quite different inks. The eighteenth century distinguished between *Marianne* and *Le Paysan* by finding 'une finesse délicate' in the one and a 'franche gaieté' in the other. The differences between them are immediately apparent to the reader who leaves Marianne to her 'babil' and turns to the refreshing bounce and energy of Jacob's adventures.

Yet though Jacob and Marianne may seem only distantly related, they are nevertheless visibly the products of the same imagination. If Marianne aspires to virtue while Jacob delights in knavish tricks, they are united in their quest to discover a means of being what they are — of securing a niche in society where they need no longer struggle to protect their fundamental goodness of heart. In spite of disparities in manner and atmosphere, the optic of both novels remains constant: a single sensibility directs the responses of two seekers after identity who never cease to observe themselves as carefully as they watch others. Marivaux's control over them is complete, and it is the measure of his powers that he was able to sustain the character of Marianne over a period of years. It goes without saying that Marivaux the novelist did not spring spontaneously to life and if we are to understand his art and purpose, we must first consider his literary beginnings.

His earliest published work was a comedy, *Le Père prudent et équitable* (Limoges, 1712), which owed less to the grand manner of 'le grand siècle' than to a grosser tradition of comic writing. The same impression of a man well-versed in secondary forms of literature emerges from his first novel, *Les Effets surprenants de la sympathie*

(1713-14), parts at least of which were written before Marivaux finally settled in Paris around the end of 1712. Its plot is impossible to summarise (Clarice loves Clorante, the hero, who loves Caliste who is held prisoner by Périandre. . .) for each new character insists on recounting highly-coloured adventures which involve more bandits, shipwrecks and abductions than are normally strewn along the path of life. Indeed, Marivaux himself seems to have experienced difficulties in distinguishing between Clorinde, Clorine and Dorine who are among an alarming number of young women who have been kidnapped or simply mislaid. Though they fall into the clutches of evil seducers, nothing terrible actually happens to them and they emerge unscathed, breathing noble sentiments about love and the respect that is owed to the fair sex. To those familiar with the importance of 'la surprise de l'amour' in Marivaux's later work, this long first novel does not live up to the promise of its title. In spite of occasional glimpses of the dawning of love and of the sudden conscious awareness of what the characters have been unconsciously feeling, *Les Effets surprenants de la sympathie* prefers the less than surprising effects of melodrama. Marivaux seems to have been content to work within the tradition of chivalrous and gallant romance which he admired in the novels of D'Urfé, Mlle de Scudéry, La Calprenède and the Cervantes of *Los Trabajos de Persiles y Sigismunda* (1617).

In one sense, *Les Effets* was ahead of its time. It has moments of dark brooding and gothic horror which prefigure the 'roman noir'. Yet as a saga of gallant love and heroic deeds, it was also anachronistic. Fiction had moved much closer to the 'récit naturel des aventures modernes' which Sorel had anticipated in his *Bibliothèque françoise* (1664) and which helps to explain the success of novels as varied as *La Princesse de Clèves* (1678), *Le Diable Boiteux* (1707) of Lesage, and Robert Chasles's neatly observed *Illustres Françoises* (1713). Marivaux appears to have had second thoughts about his novel even before it was published. In his 'Avis au Lecteur' (*1*, 3-9), he makes out a case for fiction which is curiously at odds with the tale he tells. He denounces those novels which 'ne sont que de simples aventures racontées avec une hâte qui amuse le lecteur, mais qui ne l'attendrit, ni le touche'. Unless the reader is actively involved in what he reads and is directed by a judicious use of moral and above all psychological 'réflexions', then the novel he reads will be no more than 'un amas d'actions sans âme' – a judgment which applies particularly well to *Les Effets* itself.

But the youthful Marivaux does not stop at dismissing escapist fiction: he reacts strongly against the fundamental assumptions on which contemporary critical standards were based. He rejects 'les lois stériles de l'art' and 'la régularité de nos beaux esprits savants' who 'ne lisent un livre, pour ainsi dire, qu'avec la règle et le compas dans l'esprit'. Classical art was based on the twin deities of taste and reason, both of which were designed to override the spontaneous and capture nature in formal, universal poses. Marivaux agrees that the novelist should copy nature, but he denies that 'la manière la plus délicate de composer des aventures' is to be found in the strict application of classical uniformity. Nature herself is not regular, and the reader who has an 'esprit d'honnête homme galant et aisé' will see 'natural' beauty and truth even in passages which transgress the established academic canons. He claims to write for a lady of quality well-endowed with 'ce sentiment intérieur presque toujours aussi noble que tendre, et qui seul fait juger sainement des faux ou des vrais mouvements qu'on donne au cœur'. Such a reader may lack 'érudition', but for Marivaux her ignorance of the rules of art is amply compensated by her instinctive knowledge of the human heart. He believed that women are specially gifted in the detection of emotional truth or fraud and make better judges than the 'savants jurés' who scoff at love and sneer at feelings. La Bruyère had conceded that 'le plaisir de la critique nous ôte celui d'être vivement touchés par de très belles choses'. Marivaux goes further and makes personal feeling and experience the prime element in our response to literature. When we witness 'un accident funeste qui blesse ou tue quelqu'un', we feel pity or horror. There is no reason why we should not feel as spontaneously and as authentically when we read a novel – even though we know that truth and fiction are quite distinct: 'l'âme peut s'intéresser à la lecture d'une fausse aventure, pourvu que le récit ressemble au vrai'. Though he does not define what he means by 'vrai', it clearly had little to do with the 'vraisemblable' of classical doctrine and even less with the heroic posturings of *Les Effets*. However, it would include 'une expression naïve et vraie', by which we understand a style suited to character and event, and 'un goût de sentiment' through which the reader is required to mobilise his own feelings.

At one level, the 'Avis au Lecteur' is a plea for realism of a kind frequently encountered in contemporary novels whose authors regularly sought to make fiction respectable. But at another and deeper level, Marivaux seeks to free literature from academic and ideological chains and, most significantly of all, to define our response to literature in terms of instinct and intuition. In arguing that reading a novel is neither a rational experience nor entirely an affective process, Marivaux advances a radical view of art which has subsequently been aired many times but which satisfies only liberal consciences. George Orwell echoes it, for instance, when he argues that all literary criticism is a fraud.[1] Basically, only two critical statements are possible: 'I like this book' or 'I do not like this book'. Our reasons for liking or not liking are simply a justification of an intuitive reaction. For Marivaux, our response is determined by an instinct which, as he was later to say, is 'à l'âme humaine un sentiment non déployé' (2, 71-72). The reader who does not temper his emotion with the judgment we commonly apply to people and things will fall into the error of sentimentality; the reader who does not soften his reason with feeling cannot enter the novelist's world. Reader and novelist can meet only on the common ground, not of reason and taste, but of 'le cœur' and 'l'esprit' where nature may be apprehended without undue ceremonial. Already in 1713, Marivaux was arming himself to capture truth.

The 'Avis au Lecteur' reveals the modernity of Marivaux's approach to literature. But it also allows a glimpse of his Modernist stance. His association with Fontenelle and La Motte at the *salon* of Mme de Lambert was to confirm his radical views and involve him in the 'Querelle des Anciens et des Modernes' which had begun around the end of the seventeenth century. For the 'Anciens', the writers of classical antiquity had attained a perfection which would never be equalled. Modern man was a dwarf perched on the shoulders of the giants who had preceded him, and the posture of the artist could only be one of humility and veneration: imitation of the ancients was thus the first rule of art. The Modernist party, on the other hand, while acknowledging the great contribution made by the classical world, argued that things move on: a dwarf perched on a giant's

---

[1] *Collected Essays, Journalism and Letters*, Penguin Books, 1970, IV, p.463.

shoulders can after all see further than the giant. The slavish imitation of work produced by men dead for more than two thousand years was a dereliction of each generation's duty to reflect the world as it is and not merely as it might or should be. They stood for greater freedom, and made a case for the subjective responses of the ordinary man against the learned reactions of the educated classes. In painting as well as in literature, they sought to replace the sophisticated art of the courtly tradition ('great' subjects treated in an appropriately 'noble' manner) with a more intimate and, as it turned out, a more bourgeois art. They met with strong opposition, but it was their view which prevailed in the long run.

Although Marivaux adopted a broadly Modernist stance, a more lasting mark was left on his attitudes by Mme de Lambert (1647-1733) who, from 1710 until her death, opened her *salon* to selected literati each Tuesday. Her outlook was urbane and she encouraged good conversation which reflected values (honour, delicacy, generosity) that steered a course between the patrician and the bourgeois. She turned aside from religious principles and took the view that personal and social behaviour should amount to a tolerant worldliness which had more to do with 'le bon sens' than with right reason, and less to do with passion than with an understanding heart. She recommended a newer secular morality based upon sensibility and surrounded herself with musicians, painters, actors and writers in whom she recognised a kindred humanitarianism. Mme de Lambert was no social reformer. Yet her belief that we can be good only through an educated sensibility struck a responsive chord in Marivaux which was set vibrating by the charm and kindliness of her personal conduct. He was won over completely – Marianne's benefactress, Mme de Miran, was to be modelled closely on her – and he not only adopted her basic outlook but even retained a number of expressions used by her, 'la science du cœur', for example, or the 'métaphysique' of love. In social terms, Marivaux was to prove rather less exclusive in his depiction of a new élite of sensitive, virtuous and kindly souls. For him, rank and wealth were accidents of birth, and he observed vulgarity of heart, mind and speech even in the highest levels of society. It was through the ideas and example of Mme de Lambert that Marivaux perceived how delicacy of wit and feeling could be recommended to a society dominated by strong class divisions: as time passed, he came to set the highest value upon a new aristocracy based not on title and money but upon human qualities.

Even before *Les Effets surprenants de la sympathie* appeared, Marivaux was writing *Pharsamon, ou les nouvelles folies romanesques* which he was to disown when it was published without his consent in 1737. Like Don Quixote, Pierre Bagnol, son of a country squire, has read too many heroic romances. In his pursuit of Mlle Babet, the daughter of a 'dame du village', he is abetted by a rustic servant who wipes his nose on his sleeve and cares more for his stomach than for the finer feelings. To live up to his lofty aspirations, Pierre Bagnol takes the name of Pharsamon, Babet becomes Cidalise, the valet is rechristened Cliton ('un nom d'écuyer de roman'), and together they set out to live life not as it is but as it is described in 'les anciens romans, les Amadis de Gaule, l'Arioste et tant d'autres ouvrages' (*1*, 393), prominent among which are the 'precious' novels of the seventeenth century. Though still sentimentally attached to the heroic tradition − a number of self-contained episodes revive the mood and ethos of *Les Effets* − Marivaux now exchanges one literary convention for another. In the manner of Scarron, he burlesques the elevated and mannered world of La Calprenède's *Pharamond* (1661-70) and its kind. He mocks the swoonings, sighs, tears and *langueurs* of Cidalise, Pharsamon's made-to-measure anguish, and the obligatory glades, woods and gardens where noble thoughts are expressed by noble souls: modern lovers, noted Marivaux coolly, would be more likely to chat in a room. What the characters do and feel contrasts with what they say, and Marivaux takes evident delight in showing the distance separating their 'folies romanesques' from reality. But if he constantly deflates their pretension, he also snipes at his readers, telling them to be patient, reminding his 'jeune lecteur' that tender love is far more admirable than gallant protestations, and counter-attacking those 'esprits critiques' who in their blinkered way are sure to be offended by his shocking mixture of dignity and farce and the scant respect paid to the rules of art.

Marivaux clearly enjoyed following his fancy: 'un peu de bigarrure me plaît. Suivez-moi, mon cher lecteur, à vous dire le vrai, je ne sais pas bien où je vais; mais c'est le plaisir du voyage' (*1*, 457). But though the joke of Pharsamon's incongruous adventures quickly wears thin, it is also clear that Marivaux's intentions were not entirely negative. *Pharsamon* is an attempt to define 'le vrai' of which he had spoken in the preface to *Les Effets*. Truth is not to be found in quests for glory and perfect love but in those trivialities which direct the lives we lead:

> 'ne savez-vous pas, raisonneur, que le Rien est le motif de toutes les grandes catastrophes qui arrivent parmi les hommes? Ne savez-vous pas que le Rien détermine ici l'esprit de tous les mortels; que c'est lui qui détruit les amitiés les plus fortes; qui finit les amours les plus tendres, qui les fait naître tour à tour? Que c'est le Rien qui élève celui-ci, pendant qu'il ruine la fortune de celui-là?'
> (*1*, 562)

Pharsamon may think in terms of conquest, sacrifice and honour, but Cliton's greatest adventure was to have, as a boy, hunted sparrows and stolen apples. To the reader who declares such deeds to be decidedly non-heroic, Marivaux replies that the gravest historian's account of a battle may be far more tedious than 'le simple récit de deux enfants qui jouent les yeux bandés à s'attraper l'un l'autre':

> 'La manière de raconter est toujours l'unique cause du plaisir ou de l'ennui qu'un récit inspire, et la naïveté de ces deux enfants bien écrite, et d'une manière proportionnée aux sujets qu'on expose, ne divertira pas moins l'esprit, qu'un beau récit d'une histoire grande et tragique est capable de l'élever: une pomme n'est rien; des moineaux ne sont que des moineaux; mais chaque chose dans la petitesse de son sujet est capable de beautés, d'agréments: il n'y a plus que l'espèce de différence' (*1*, 602)

In other words, Marivaux urges the demystification of the novel. Its values were to be demythologised and its characters demoted. It is a plea for a simpler realism, for the elevation of ordinary life and ordinary people to a place of seriousness in literature.

But if he rejected the inflated manner and assumptions of the courtly and heroic tradition, Marivaux was obviously fascinated by the potential of a form of writing which had yet to be exploited. From La Calprenède and Mlle de Scudéry, he learned that good story-telling is inseparable from the communication of values. Though their analyses were no longer seasonable, the problem was not to eschew analysis but rather to find ways of expressing less exalted truths and a more accessible view of human nature. If satire is a barbed form of respect, then Marivaux was still drawn by the idealism of the novels he burlesques. But this idealism was directed less towards a specifically aristocratic imperative than towards the wish to paint a faithful picture of modern man in his dealings with himself and with others. In *Pharsamon*, he experimented with techniques which were to remain an integral part of his approach as a novelist. In particular, he intervenes as author in his third-person narrative — thus anticipating that double perspective which emerges from the observations which the older Marianne and Jacob make on their younger selves — and adopts a style which broke with formal elegance and the abstract in favour of a more graphic, colloquial and vigorous means of expression.

While Marivaux was quite serious in this new view of the novel, it is also evident that his Modernism lacked missionary zeal: he was later to admit frankly to being 'neutre sur tout culte littéraire' (*2*, 159). He was attracted far more by 'le plaisir du voyage' than by matters of theory and clearly surrendered to an obvious delight in story-telling. He followed his imagination where it led him and *Pharsamon*, like *La Voiture embourbée* which followed it, is a mixture of heroic and mock-heroic, comedy and tragedy, realism and melodrama — in a word, of cliché and originality which constituted that 'bigarrure' which so pleased his eye. *La Voiture embourbée* (1714) begins with a coaching accident and a realistic account of the narrator's fellow passengers and their arrival at a country tavern where they pass the night. To while away the time, they take turns in telling a 'roman impromptu' which gravitates once more towards the pastoral, the mock-heroic and even to a fashionable 'féerie' to which Marivaux was subsequently to return, not in his novels, but in certain of his plays.

If the first chapter of *La Voiture embourbée* anticipates the genre painting of Marivaux's later manner, the rest shows him both exploiting and satirising the narrative clichés of genteel fiction. But though be believed that the novel should reflect the lifestyle of a new generation which was witnessing the shift of French cultural life away from the court of Versailles towards Paris and its less aristocratic values, he did not limit his ambitions to any one literary form. In his still youthful mood of exploration, he turned next to a more conventional expression of the burlesque. His *Homère travesti, ou l'Iliade en vers burlesques* (1716), which was widely viewed as a defence of Modernism, revived the approach of Scarron who, in his *Virgile travesti* (1649-59), had retold the *Aeneid* in incongrous terms of farce and vulgarity. Marivaux's attempt to ridicule the high regard in which Homer was held by the 'Anciens' proved, however, to be hesitant and uncertain, and did not amount to much of an advertisement for the Modernist cause. However, a second parody – of Fénelon's much admired edifying novel, *Les Aventures de Télémaque* – was to be rather more than a satire of the epic style or even of Fénelon's patrician teaching.

Of *Le Télémaque travesti*, only a few parts appeared in 1736 when Marivaux disclaimed it, doubtless embarrassed to be confronted with a work of his youth at a time when the 'guerre homérique' was long over. Télémaque's adventures are set in France at the time of Louis XIV's wars, and Brideron, a 'jeune bourgeois de campagne', relives his hero's life which is here transposed into the farmyards and villages of contemporary France. Though the approach recalls *Pharsamon*, Marivaux sustains his comic-epic vein much more successfully and in particular endows Brideron with certain picaresque characteristics which enable him to comment freely upon men and manners. More at home with prose than verse and giving a looser rein to his personal observation and experience, Marivaux provides a tale of epic deeds among the chickens which affords much good-humoured, tolerant, amused – and amusing – reflections on life.

*Le Télémaque travesti* appears to have exhausted Marivaux's early interest in the novel, which had given more signs of promise than real achievement. He disappoints, perhaps, because he had yet to resolve the tensions between the masculine/feminine poles of his sensibility – the sturdy *Télémaque*, for instance, as against the more melting *Les Effets* – which Frédéric Deloffre has defined (*1*, 1091). But a more immediate reason may be that for all his arguments in favour of 'le vrai' and of a manner of writing which appealed simultaneously to 'le cœur' and 'l'esprit', he persisted in drawing less upon life than upon literature. His terms of reference were almost entirely literary, his vision swinging predictably from one convention (epic and romance) to another (parody and comic realism). Although he had composed five long narratives by the age of twenty-six or twenty-seven, Marivaux the novelist, in spite of a quantity of theorising, had yet to find his way.

Though he did not return to the novel until the late 1720s (the first part of *Marianne* was approved by the censor in April 1728), he continued to search for a means of presenting truth plain and un-coloured. In 1717, he began contributing to the *Mercure de France*, then regarded as the house-journal of Modernism, a series of *Lettres sur les habitants de Paris* which characterise classes and types with shrewdness and humour: the first, for example, describes the popu-lace in terms which anticipate the 'scène du cocher' in *Marianne* or Jacob's rescue of Dorsan in *Le Paysan*. As a journalist, Marivaux threw off the literary chains that bound him and, following in the steps of Addison and Steele whose *Spectator* (1711-12) was admired throughout Europe, he simply looked around and reported what he saw.

In his journalism, he made the most of a natural talent for anec-dote. But he also exploited a useful ability to extract striking thoughts from the most trivial 'Riens' and to develop them into amused and sometimes paradoxical observations on life. As *Le Spectateur français* (25 issues, 1721-24), he confessed that 'je suis né de manière que tout me devient une matière de réflexion' (*2*, 117). At last he was learning that life is more varied and more curious than literature and now began to prefer 'toutes les idées fortuites que le hasard nous donne à celles que la recherche la plus ingénieuse pourrait nous four-nir dans le travail' (*2*, 116-7). In an article in the *Mercure* of March 1719, he had already reacted strongly against the sublime in art, and had redefined the search for 'la clarté du discours' not as the attempt to express meaning through the standardised language of good taste but as a process of suggesting a whole thought by means of an image or even an unexpected turn of phrase: the 'vivacité' of the idea is transmitted by association and not by terms which have a single, dic-tionary definition (*2*, 52). In other words, he saw the advantages of his 'libertinage d'idées' and was consciously refining a style which, if irregular by contemporary standards, was to become the perfect in-strument of self-expression. And all the while he was observing his own reactions and personality which alone gave unity and consisten-

cy to his apparently random thoughts. As one of his alleged corres-
pondents remarks:

> 'Dans tout le cours de mes aventures, j'ai été mon propre specta-
> teur, comme le spectateur des autres; je me suis connu autant
> qu'il est possible de se connaître; ainsi, c'est du moins un homme
> que j'ai developpé, et quand j'ai comparé cet homme aux autres,
> ou les autres à lui, j'ai cru voir que nous nous ressemblions
> presque tous.' (*2*, 232)

By being himself − consciously himself − Marivaux believed that he
could open the hearts and minds of his readers.

Marivaux's journals − in addition to the *Spectateur français* there
were *L'Indigent philosophe* (7 issues, 1727) and the eleven numbers
of *Le Cabinet du Philosophe* (1734) − may be underplanned; they
may start more anecdotes than they finish; they may even express
views (on charity, women, morals, religion, the egoism of the rich
and so on) which though perceptive are tentative and unsystematic.
But they encouraged him to look around him and to observe what
he saw. They gave him confidence in his judgements, cured him of
literature and helped him to develop an independent and natural
style through which he expressed a new kind of 'clarté': a clear perception of men and women going about their business in the world
in which he himself lived. He did not seek to be the chronicler of his
age, nor the recorder of the 'fait divers', but the historian of 'le Rien'.
From a trivial incident, a fleeting fashion, a chance remark, a sudden
thought, he filtered his observations through his own sensibility and
reduced the malice, generosity, folly, kindness, pretension and stupi-
dity he witnessed to a coherent and timeless picture of his contemporaries. His account of society subordinates politics and broad social
or theological issues to the morality of everyday action, for at the
centre of his picture of men and manners was a lasting concern for
human values.

Marivaux's experience as a journalist completed his long appren-
ticeship as a novelist. Meanwhile, after his marriage in 1717 to
Colombe Bollogne who died six years later, after losing most of his
money when John Law's Louisiana Bubble burst in 1720 and after
an abortive attempt to complete his legal training, he set about mak-

ing a career in the theatre where he had taken his first literary steps in 1712. It was not until he was established as a successful playwright that he once more turned to the novel.

Though Marianne was born 'pour avoir des aventures' (*4*, 370) which she delights in relating, her freest rein is given to her insatiable curiosity about human nature. She looks long and hard at those whom she encounters, interpreting their gestures and facial expressions, and translating what they say into what they really mean. Yet she is constantly aware that her efforts to get to the truth about people can never succeed: 'on ne saurait rendre en entier ce que sont les personnes... Ce sont des objets de sentiment si compliqués et d'une netteté si délicate qu'ils se brouillent dès que ma réflexion s'en mêle; je ne sais par où les prendre pour les exprimer' (*4*, 170). Jacob, a no less compulsive scrutineer, experiences similar problems: 'ce ne serait jamais fait si on voulait tout dire, et peut-être qu'on n'en viendrait pas à bout. Est-ce qu'on peut dire tout ce qu'on sent?' (*6*, 137). The difficulty of their enterprise is extreme. For not only are the 'objets de sentiment' themselves complex and constantly changing, but our view of them is determined by the 'réflexion' of the head and the feelings of the heart, which are no less intricate and unstable: other people, objectively and subjectively, both as they are and as we see them, defy analysis. For Jacob and Marianne, it is a practical problem, since their progress depends on the accurate assessment of other people who may help or hinder them. But it was also an aesthetic problem for Marivaux, who was only too well aware of the irreducible ambiguities of human nature: 'les hommes sont bien au-dessus des livres qu'ils font' (*4*, 170).

While Marivaux was intrigued by certain abstract problems of this sort (he pursued a number of metaphysical questions with comparable detachment), he was never paralysed by them. *Le Paysan parvenu* may seem to place less emphasis on analysis than *La Vie de Marianne*, but each in its own way expresses Marivaux's wish to 'paint nature' in the appropriate terms. Experience had shown him that novelists had failed to be true when they set exceptional characters in exceptional circumstances and required them to struggle with pirates rather than with 'le Rien', which is a much more formidable oppon-

ent. He had also learnt to mistrust his own facility as a story-teller —
Marianne too sets more store by her 'babil' than by the 'simple récit
des faits' (*4*, 252) — because a preoccupation with mere narrative
turns drama into melodrama and converts the narrator into an atti-
tudiniser. As 'le Spectateur français', Marivaux strove to write not as
an author who has opinions to order but as a man whose views
spring naturally out of what he observes (*2*, 114). If Marianne denies
that her memoirs are fiction, she does so not merely to suggest that
they were true, but to insist on the freshness and individuality of her
observations: 'ce n'est point un auteur, c'est une femme qui pense'
(*4*, 85). If Jacob's life contains more adventures and fewer reflections, he too filters his experiences through 'cet art de lire dans
l'esprit des gens et de débrouiller leurs sentiments'(*6*, 91). Marivaux's
concern was not with events, crises and high drama, but with psychological analysis. His novels are a denial of 'le romanesque' and a pro-
clamation of a personal, independent and non-standardised vision.

Of course, no artist ever quite breaks with tradition, and
Marivaux's pursuit of human truth is strongly marked by his admiration for seventeenth-century moralists like La Bruyère and La
Rochefoucauld, who sought to reduce humanity to a gallery of types
and a collection of aphorisms. Tervire describes her uncle ('c'était
un de ces hommes ordinaires que. . .' (*4*, 385)), in terms which are less
individual than general. Jacob too seeks to relate his character
sketches to broad categories: Mme de Fécour's sister belongs with
'ces femmes laides' who use religion as a means of discounting their
personal unattractiveness (*6*, 221), and even Mme de Ferval has a
'caractère' which though singular 'n'est pas si rare qu'on ne pense'
(*6*, 169). Marianne's numerous 'portraits' apply a formula (she
moves from 'le physique' and 'la physionomie' to 'l'esprit' and 'le
cœur' before ending on 'l'âme') which imposes uniform standards
of judgment on universal types — even though Marivaux may work
from specific models as in the case of Mme de Miran who was based
on Mme de Lambert, or Mme Dorsin who was inspired by Mme de
Tencin, or the President who is an idealised version of Fleury.
Though Marianne's formal analyses are deft and distinctive, they
tend to classify eternal 'caractères' whose reality depends less on
their particular qualities than on the relation they have to classical
psychology. Her 'portraits' not only halt the action, sometimes for

pages on end, but state in abstract terms what is better shown through dialogue, gesture and action. Marivaux's taste for them gives his narratives a certain static quality which runs counter to his obvious wish to show real people in real situations. There are moments when even his main characters seem threatened by stereotyping. Jacob ranks himself with 'tous les jeunes gens de province et de ma sorte' (*6*, 239) as if to imply that he is one of many; Cathos reminds Marianne that girls like her usually stay 'sur le pavé: on vous en montrera mille comme vous qui y sont' (*4*, 280). Yet Marivaux succeeds in interesting us precisely because he could not sustain them as mere 'caractères'. They regularly escape his universalising and turn into disconcerting and unpredictable individuals. Even M. de Climal, who begins as a hypocrite in the mould of Tartuffe, gradually acquires depth and even, in the end, a certain dignity. Marivaux's residual sympathy with the aims of the classical moralists led him to minimise the particular in favour of the general. But his loyalty weakened before his temperamental fascination not with common denominators but with distinctions and differences − with what makes human beings separate and unique rather than with what makes them the same. His interest in 'caractères' was backward-looking; his delight in personal foibles led him to a recognisably modern approach to psychology.

Structurally, Marivaux's presentation of character reflects the gradual erosion of his classical allegiances. He retained the set-piece 'portrait' for characters of moral distinction and/or rank (the two do not always overlap). Even Jacob takes to the traditional categories, classifying Agathe as 'amoureuse' rather than 'tendre' (*6*, 92) and Mme de Fécour as being all 'sens' and no 'sentiment' (*6*, 169); he too uses the formal study (the longest being that of Mme de Ferval (*6*, 136-8) ) as a starting point for general comments about egoism or pride. But it is Marianne who is most given to these full and abstract equivalents of the painter's still-life. She works steadily inward from her under-personalised descriptions of face and figure towards those characteristics of heart, mind and soul which have more to do with universals than with specifically individual qualities. But even she speaks of the difficulty of assembling a 'caractère', which is 'un ouvrage sans fin' (*4*, 215) and, confessing that 'tous ces portraits me coûtent' (*4*, 206), she sometimes wearies of the effort. Thus after sketching Mlle de Fare's 'physionomie vive, rusée et non maligne' in terms that are more moral than graphic, she stops with the comment that her subject will be revealed 'par les choses que je dirai dans la suite' (*4*, 240). Marianne regularly complements her static portraits by showing how people behave, speak and act, and converts her stationary types into animated figures: Marivaux not only carved statues, he also made them move.

For secondary characters, however, he was much readier to provide brief thumb-nail sketches — age, physical appearance, personal eccentricities — which are altogether more factual and pictorial. If his portraits describe even physical traits in moral terms ('un air de franchise', 'une mine consolante', 'une expression vive et badine'), these shorter sketches (of the abbess, the 'officier' or Dursan *père* (*4*, 272, 372, 445)) spring off the page enlivened by a near Dickensian touch of whimsy: Tervire's suitor is pious and asthmatic in equal amounts (*4*, 410-11) and there is something almost grotesque about Mlle Cathos's wide mouth and long nose (*4*, 292) or the lantern-jawed *spectre* whose fingers 'ne finissaient point' and whose name is less memorable than 'la singularité de sa figure' (*4*, 265, 295). Jacob, as befits his wide-eyed naiveté, has an even stronger relish for visual oddities — like Mme de Fécour's 'furieuse gorge' (*6*, 167) or his witness's ill-fitting wig and amazing cuffs (*6*, 110). But he is equally fond of portraying people through their gestures, dress and speech. As a result, Mme d'Alain is easier to imagine than Mme de Miran, and the gruff M. Bono, though he has an abstract 'mine de grandeur' which is difficult to visualise, is fixed firmly in our minds by his staccato delivery. Jacob in particular fills the background to his story with many such vivid 'impressions' not of moral abstractions but of physical presences. The effect is to bring his world to bustling life: Agathe's unpleasant character emerges naturally from her behaviour, while Jacob's first mistress is seen through her peculiar lifestyle and M. Doucin condemns himself out of his own mouth. It should not be thought, however, that Jacob has a monopoly of this more direct and dramatic method of showing character. Marianne offers a lively glimpse of her bourgeois suitor and stands back to allow his words and actions to convey his unfortunate manner and tasteless 'façons' (*4*, 281-6). If Jacob describes Mlle Habert in largely physical terms ('succulemment nourrie... vermeille... cinquant-

aine... écharpe... fraîche... ragoûtante' (*6*, 54-5)) before we see
her character revealed through her attitudes and conduct, Marianne
paints an even more vivid picture of Mme de Fare, a 'petite femme
brune, assez ronde, très laide, qui avait le visage large et carré, avec
de petits yeux noirs, qui d'abord paraissaient vifs, mais qui n'étaient
que curieux et inquiets'. The classical moralist in Marivaux may have
tempted him to class her as a type (she is one of those people 'dont
l'esprit n'est en mouvement que par pure disette d'idées'), but he
immediately rescues her from abstraction by an image which draws
her back into the tangible world: 'Je les compare à un homme qui
passerait sa vie à se tenir à sa fenêtre' (*4*, 237).

Marivaux's handling of his characters thus moves steadily away
from the 'portrait moral' towards briefer impressions which are less
abstract, more vivid and occasionally even caricatural. But both are
consolidated by a more vigorous sense of drama. If Marivaux the
moralist provides complete and detailed analyses, Marivaux the novelist invites us to look through his narrators' eyes and see what they
see. He keeps the front of his stage filled with well-defined human
figures who come and go, but the movement we observe there is frequently deceptive. When Marianne is interviewed by Mme de Miran
and the abbess, she is struck by those 'apparences' and 'superficies'
of which she is both victim and beneficiary: she is misled just as in
turn 'mon habit les trompait' (*4*, 158). Marivaux describes the ex-
terior of his characters in the hope that we will proceed beyond
appearances to the unmasked human truth — that we will not merely see but see through. For Jacob and Marianne, human beings are
transparent and, fifty years before Lavater tried to justify the reading of character from the interpretation of physiognomies, Marivaux
tests to the limit our belief that our true natures are written on our
faces.

He describes faces which reassure, win hearts, inspire confidence
and undo evil report; they betray surprise, hidden thoughts, base
intentions, cruelty and natural kindness. The human face is used as
the subtlest form of non-verbal communication: it is more immediate, more comprehensive and more reliable than words. It takes
Jacob one glance to know Mme D'Orville: 'c'était, pour ainsi dire,
une âme qu'on voyait sur ce visage' (*6*, 189). Marianne recognises
Mme de Miran's understanding in her 'regard' (*4*, 156) and sees

'honnêteté' in the eyes of Mlle de Fare (*4*, 239). She pursues her love for Valville through 'le langage des yeux' (*4*, 244) and it is by his 'physionomie autrefois si pénétrée et si attendrie' that she knows instinctively that he has betrayed her with Varthon (*4*, 353). Marianne, Tervire and Jacob trust implicitly in such signals, which they decode with unerring accuracy. When they are embarrassed or discomfited, they in turn feel as exposed to the world as they are to the reader, who is made party to their every thought. But they are also aware that faces tell as many lies as tongues. Agathe is born with a face which belies her character – 'la nature fait assez souvent ces tricheries-là' (*6*, 52), notes Jacob – while other faces are turned into masks which conceal the truth, as in the case of the evil-thinking bigot who 'ne sortait qu'avec une tristesse dévote et précieuse sur le visage' (*6*, 180). Interested parties, too, readily exploit the lesson of a particular cast of features. The abbess, rubbing her hands at the prospect of a rich addition to her establishment, confidently predicts to Marianne that 'votre vocation est écrite sur votre visage' (*4*, 159), while M. Doucin, anxious for his own position, warns the Habert sisters against 'la mine d'un honnête homme' which Jacob presents to them (*6*, 71). Marianne and Jacob, unlike the more trusting Tervire, make few mistakes. With deadly efficiency, they strip their victims of their cultivated manner and social personalities. They are endowed with an instinctive lucidity compounded of affective intuitions and a few simple moral standards: they warm to generosity, kindness and honesty, and they recoil from hypocrisy, self-interest and the abuse of rank and power. Those who live in harmony with their inoffensive natures – Mme de Miran, Mlle de Fare, Villot the peasant and M. Bono, for example – have no cause to hide their faces because their charity is sincere. But those who, like M. de Climal, Agathe or Mme de Ferval, don masks to disguise their nasty schemes, stand guilty of duplicity. They are judged but they are not punished. For if Marivaux's heroes lack forgiveness, they are without vindictiveness. Like Voltaire, they merely defend themselves when attacked.

And sometimes they defend themselves too well, for they too turn false faces to the world. If Jacob has every reason to be pleased with his face (*6*, 103-1), he regularly adjusts his speech to suit his circumstances. Hauled before the magistrate, his deliberately 'naïve'

turns of phrase are calculated to win the sympathy of his listeners
(*6*, 146); in the coach to Versailles, he is careful to say nothing 'qui
sentît le fils de fermier de campagne' (*6*, 177); with Mlle Habert he
exaggerates his country accent which she finds so attractive (*6*, 90).
Marianne is no more defenceless than Jacob and yet she is capable
of stating, with every appearance of sincerity, that she is 'une
malheureuse orpheline que Dieu, qui est le maître, a abandonnée
à toutes les misères imaginables' (*4*, 302). Both may watch others
but they too are watched – by those they meet, by their older
selves and of course by the reader. They seem far removed from the
linear uniformity of classical psychology, for they are ambiguous,
secret and opaque.

Marianne, for all her independence of spirit, is the beneficiary of
appearances. From what begins as merely circumstantial evidence
emerge 'des indices presque certains' (*4*, 297) that she is nobly born.
These 'indices' stem less from her reassurance that her suspicions
were in fact true (*4*, 51) than from the impression she makes on
others. Their reactions to what she seems to be allow her to claim a
matching nobility of soul. She constantly reminds us (as though we
might not notice) that her heart is 'bon', 'fin' and 'délicat'. She taxes
herself with vanity but does so with such modesty that we are tempted to excuse her. After all, others find her just as noble as she tells
us she is. As a child, the villagers treated her like 'une petite princesse' (*4*, 53) and M. de Climal needs but a glimpse of her face to be
'porté à croire qu'elle a de la naissance' (*4*, 64). The circumstances of
her birth, which she puts to excellent use, draw respect, but her
'façons douces et avenantes' regularly earn ' la bienveillance de tout
le monde' (*4*, 221). Even her enemies find her irresistible: like
Goldsmith's churchgoers who came to scoff but remained to pray,
the hardest hearts melt before her. Climal yields and the President
cannot but find in her favour. The abbess pays fulsome tribute to
her merit and graces (*4*, 275) and even Varthon repects her calm dignity and upright heart (*4*, 370). Mme de Miran never wearies of ex-
tolling her artless and disinterested nature and Mme Dorsin's first
impression could not be more favourable: 'en vérité, je ne sache
point de figure plus aimable, ni d'un air plus noble' (*4*, 174). By the
time Tervire points out that 'un caractère excellent, un esprit raisonnable et une âme vertueuse valent bien des parents' (*4*, 379),

Marianne's nobility of soul is so firmly established that the confirmation of her noble birth will surely prove to be a mere formality.

Yet she does not always behave nobly. Her attitude towards M. de Climal is equivocal. She accepts his gifts, feigning ignorance of his designs, because her vanity is stronger than her virtue. She might feel a twinge of shame, but she finds excellent reasons for acting against her conscience and shows a 'souplesse admirable pour être innocent d'une sottise qu'on a envie de faire' (*4*, 74), as the narrator wryly puts it. She might feel uncomfortable parading in her finery before Toinon, but she wears her 'belles hardes' to church where she ensures that she is seen to the best advantage. Her coquetry is at this stage doubtless an aspect of her 'vanité novice' (*4*, 84), yet even as she displays her ankle to Valville for medical purposes, we are made aware that she is more calculating than she believes. The coming of love may enable her to see herself and others more clearly — 'les tendresses du neveu, jeune, aimable et galant, m'avaient appris à voir l'oncle tel qu'il était' (*4*, 125) — but it fails to modify her constitutional deviousness in the pursuit of her own interest. When she realises what Valville means to her, 'les affaires de mon coeur' take precedence over her plight (*4*, 142) and yet, though matured by love, she continues to find good reasons for behaving like the schemer her enemies see in her. A visit to Père Vincent is perhaps a logical step, but it also satisfies her vanity: she has an excuse for wearing her pretty clothes for another hour or two. Ironically, this immodest desire to be seen (and to be seen at her best) proves to be not her undoing but her salvation. Though there is nothing calculated in the despair which overcomes her in the convent church, it is certainly enhanced by her youth, beauty and fine dress which attract the attention of Mme de Miran. If with time her vanity assumes subtler forms of 'amour-propre', her commitment to truth seems more a policy than a state of mind. When Mme de Miran expresses her concern for Valville's infatuation with an unknown 'grisette', Marianne wrestles with her conscience before confessing that she is the shop-girl in question: but instead of earning the displeasure of her benefactress, her honesty simply increases her stock. In the same way she tells Mme de Miran, against Valville's advice, that Mme de Fare has rooted out the secret of her birth, and her reputation for virtue reaches new heights.

In the event, the practice of virtue promotes Marianne's interests – even though her actions, judged from without, do not always seem self-interested. She may not set out deliberately to mislead: indeed, she regards deception as being not only dishonest but vulgar. But she wears an air of guile which is part of that mixture of goodness and pride which makes her character so complex.

Of course, there is ample evidence that her goodness of heart is genuine. Her modest disclaimers may not always carry conviction, but her instinct, which is her constant guide, is reassuring. She is constantly drawn towards 'l'honnêteté' through an alliance of 'sagesse naturelle' and 'amour-propre' (4, 202). Yet she is never reluctant to publicise the direction her instinct prompts her to take. She projects the most favourable image of herself because she believes (rightly, for the most part) that her qualities when properly packaged will help her achieve justifiable ends – love, or the social esteem to which her natural nobility entitles her. But if her ends are respectable, her means seem less so. On several occasions she tells her story in styles adopted to the psychology of her listeners (Mme de Miran, the President, Varthon, etc.) and each time succeeds in manipulating her audience in accordance with her purposes. She may not be ambitious for money or status in themselves, but she has a fierce desire to achieve a position in society which is compatible with the idea she has of her own qualities. We may find it possible to excuse her on the grounds of youth, of the dislike most of her aquaintance show for virtue, or of the difficulties facing a pretty orphan in a naughty world. Yet though she is disarmingly self-critical, accusations of hypocrisy and double-dealing are not easily dismissed. She admits to being 'plusieurs femmes en une' (4, 83) and the old head she wears on her young shoulders may well seem at times to be too clever by half. She is persecuted and betrayed. But she also resists, and she resists so well that not only does she win her battles but humiliates her enemies. She manages it through the practice of virtue, though when we recall that those who are in a position to help her are ready to give practical rewards for goodness, her virtue itself may seem calculated – a strategy rather than an instinct. Her responses are rarely transparent and in her the victim is not always distinguishable from the predator.

Jacob, on the other hand, gives every appearance of being a deliberate cheat. He knows that his greatest assets are a handsome face and a ready tongue and he wastes no opportunity to ingratiate himself with anyone who might assist his upward progress. He lacks Marianne's scruples and is not so sensitive that events, however serious or moving, prevent him from getting outside a square meal. He has the healthy appetites and cheerful amoralism of the picaresque hero whose sole function is to survive by his wits.[2] He too calculates his public image, modulating his accent and speaking not truth itself but rather 'comme on dit la vérité' (*6*, 56). To Mlle Habert he plays the naive and attentive lover; to Catherine he makes the cheeky and slightly risqué remarks which she obviously expects; to Mme de Ferval he poses as the simple, lusty youth she wants. With each new female acquaintance, he senses that there is 'une assez belle carrière ouverte à mes galanteries' (*6*, 92-93): even as he defends himself to the magistrate, he varies his voice and manner in a way which wins the hearts of the ladies present. He makes much of his 'franchise', yet his words and actions measure sincerity in carefully judged quantities. His delight in his new possessions would seem to define him as a 'beau garçon' who gets on in life by using women. Of course, like Marianne, he defends himself well. He makes the most of his solid family background; he implies that since all around him are uniformly hypocritical and immoral, he would be a fool not to turn their vices against them; and not least, he himself mocks his youthful brashness and thus anticipates our criticisms. Yet overall, just as Marianne projects an image of virtue under siege, Jacob appears to be the 'fripon' he is frequently accused of being.

Paradoxically, there is much more moral consistency in him than his actions would suggest. It is not exactly true, for instance, that he succeeds through women. Cupidity gets the better of honour in the matter of Geneviève's money, but Geneviève is far from being his innocent and defenceless prey. He may appear to take advantage of Mlle Habert, but his conduct is motivated less by an acquisitive spirit than by feelings which, though he does not understand them fully,

---

[2]  The picaresque novel, popular in Spain in the sixteenth and seventeenth centuries, chronicled the adventures of the low-born, shrewd and sometimes endearing *pícaro* as he struggled to make his way towards fortune and success. Normally written in the first person, its mixture of adventure, realism and moral comment was to be much imitated in European literature — in England by Defoe and, most obviously, by Lesage in France.

are quite genuine. Neither Mme de Ferval nor Mme de Fécour make him richer and his entry into society is engineered not with a sinecure provided by M. de Fécour but by his rescue of Dorsan. Most of his actions are instinctive rather than calculated and his instincts, like Marianne's, are fundamentally good. If she is less admirable than she seems, Jacob is more estimable than he appears to be.

If he treats Geneviève shabbily, he is the first to admit it, for he is 'chicané par son cœur'. If he is relieved by the timely death of his master, he feels uncomfortable and tries to justify his callousness (6, 50). Any doubts we have about him are modified by the genuine compassion he feels for his impoverished mistress who assesses him fairly if a little prophetically: 'tu as un bon cœur qui ne demeurera pas sans récompense' (6, 52). It is a comparable impulse which leads him to help the faltering Mlle Habert on the Pont-Neuf. He quickly falls into a role to suit his circumstances, but he is no more hypocritical than the Habert sisters who should know better, and he is no more of a fraud than M. Doucin whom he exposes. It is only half-consciously that his behaviour towards Mlle Habert grows bolder as the 'bonne fortune' he associates with her proves to be not money but love. But once their feelings have been reciprocated, Jacob is quick enough to seize his opportunity to cut a dash as M. de la Vallée. What he feels for her may not be love (6, 90), yet he is certain that his affection for her is genuine — even if it is based on no more than gratitude. Even so, he is able to protest his sincere love sincerely: 'en lui parlant ainsi je ne sentis rien en moi qui démentît mon discours'. If he deceives her — 'je tâchai d'avoir l'air et le ton tranchant' — he also deceives himself: 'je fis si bien que j'en fus dupe moi-même' (6, 96). Indeed, he is 'étonné de l'aimer tant' (6, 97). But whatever the true nature of his feelings for her, they are untainted by thoughts of gain. He is well able to distinguish between love and money ('mon cœur n'est pas une marchandise' (6, 97)) and though he takes pleasure in his new-found wealth, he is not so astute nor so long-sighted that he can carry off a swindle as easily as he succeeds in matters of the heart. M. Doucin gets the better of him and even the grocer insults him. 'Il faudrait avoir un furieux fonds d'effronterie pour tenir bon contre de certaines choses, et je n'étais né que hardi, et point effronté' (6, 107). Jacob emerges more as an opportunist than as a conspirator.

Of course, Jacob, like Marianne, has more than one face. Taking his cue from circumstances rather than from a concerted plan of campaign, he sizes up the opposition and leaves the rest to his instinct for survival. If he adopts an appropriate stance when confronting his judges, he does so quite intuitively: 'on agit dans mille moments en conséquence d'idées confuses qui viennent je ne sais comment, qui vous mènent' (6, 126). And even during his interview with Mme de Ferval, when his vanity prompts him to follow her unkind lead about Mlle Habert, he protests that he was a weak and inexperienced youth, not an 'effronté fripon' (6, 132) – and we are tempted to agree. His intentions towards his new benefactress are vague (he has no 'dessein déterminé' (6, 135)) and he is moved more by her flattery than by any thought of self-advancement, though he confuses respect, the 'étonnement pour mon aventure' and his 'ivresse de vanité' with love. At such moments, Jacob's better nature seems endangered by self-deception. Yet his capacity for disinterested action and feeling is unimpaired: he intervenes in the murder and though he is brought close to death he ends by feeling compassion for the convicted prisoner. Nor is he so far gone that he can suppress a pang of conscience that Mlle Habert should praise the 'generous' help given by Mme de Ferval in securing his release.

As M. de la Vallée, Jacob is overcome by an almost endearing self-satisfaction. 'Gonflé d'amour-propre, et tout ébouli de mon mérite' (6, 166), he refuses Mme de Ferval's offer of money which collides with the view he is acquiring of himself. But however pleased with himself he might be, he grows more vulnerable, not less: at Versailles, he feels humiliated. Yet it is precisely at this moment when his newly acquired social position is worthless that Jacob, thrown back on the devices of his nature, reveals himself in the most disinterested light. Though he is subconsciously drawn to Mme D'Orville, he refuses the position which he is offered out of a sense of decency. It is an action which gives the lie to his image as a man determined to succeed at any cost: the human sympathy he once showed to his unfortunate mistress has turned into something which closely resembles chivalry. The further he progresses (and he notes the stages of his development with care), the less of a *pícaro* he becomes. His defeat at the hands of the nobleman who calls him 'Mons Jacob' is a profound humiliation, for as M. de la Vallée he has finer feelings but fewer ready answers. But his new awareness of himself also permits him to see that what he feels for the unmasked Mme de Ferval is not love but lust (*6*, 211). Jacob lacked the 'effronterie' which would have made him ruthless; M. de la Vallée lacks the 'insolence' which would have answered insult with insult. He retreats not because his vanity is injured but out of self-respect (*6*, 226): he has a clearer notion of honour than either of his tormentors and it now becomes the principle which directs his actions. This 'agréable, métamorphose' from peasant to the 'honnête homme' which we suspect he will become, leads him to set an even lower value on money and ambition. 'Sans hésiter et sans aucune réflexion' (*6*, 227), he plunges into the brawl which threatens Dorsan.' 'Je n'attendais rien de cette aventure-ci, et ne pensais pas qu'elle dût me rapporter autre chose que l'honneur d'avoir fait une bonne action. Ce fut l'origine de ma fortune' (*6*, 232-3). With Dorsan, he no longer has to cheat: he ceases to pretend to be what he is not, relies on his natural dignity and, far from adopting yet another false tone of voice, discovers that he is accepted for what he is. It is in this aristocratic company of men that Jacob at last begins to feel at ease. His natural capacity for disinterested action has not changed — it was in the same spirit that he comforted his mistress and rescued Mlle Habert. It is simply that Jacob seems on the verge of being accepted for his natural qualities which he has neither to defend nor explain. He is no wealthier than before he met D'Orville or Dorsan, but he has gained a foothold in a world which recognises his merits. Jacob never was a knave, though circumstances and his naïveté made him seem one. At the point where we leave him, he is on the way to becoming a hero.

In comparison, Tervire — the nun who sets out to show Marianne that life with parents can be even more trying than life without a family — is exactly what she seems to be. She is sensitive and resilient like Marianne, but she lacks her vanity and self-awareness just as she has neither Jacob's charm nor his perspicacity. If Marianne and Jacob rarely reveal their true feelings, Tervire has little control over her face. When she learns that the pious *abbé* is in fact a seducer, she flees from Mme de Sainte-Hermières: 'je croyais avoir le visage aussi changé que l'esprit', and she needs a moment alone 'pour prendre une mine où l'on ne connût rien' (*4*, 406). Tervire is much more obviously a victim, for she is, with a few exceptions, without suspicion of other people's motives. She sees the villainy of Mme de Sainte-Hermières only when its effects are made public, and she has no idea that Brunon is not the sweet, much-wronged creature she seems to be. Her myopia makes other people unpredictable in a way that does not happen in Marianne's or Jacob's memoirs. Unlike them, she is frequently surprised to learn that her judgement of people, which is based on her trusting heart and not upon shrewdness of head, is often premature or mistaken. She eventually acquires a degree of lucidity but her experiences make our view of Marianne and Jacob even more enigmatic. If we are made uncomfortable by the ease with which they defend themselves, Tervire's defeats demonstrate that goodness alone is not enough and that a hint of toughness in defending her interests would have made her less vulnerable. Though it is unlikely that Marivaux intended his three major characters to be complementary in any systematic way, they represent between them aspects of human nature which he evidently believed to be of permanent value. Tervire's goodness contrasts with Marianne's well-defined delicacy while Jacob's essential good-heartedness emerges only when his sensuality is disciplined by his growing sense of honour. If virtue is to triumph, then is must be militant not meek.

If Marivaux's novels thus show ideal values at odds with the real world, similar tensions between the abstract and the concrete are visible in his presentation of character, which is a mixture of the general and the particular. His 'portraits' show human and moral qualities in their universal form, but the characters who scamper across his pages are also individualised and elusive. We hear their words, witness their action and see their faces, yet the meaning of what they do or say is not always clear. For much occurs beneath the surface. When Marianne sees Paris for the first time, she does not, as we might expect, describe the streets or the people: she talks of her inner 'surprise', her 'mouvements d'âme' and of half-understood emotions. Often an unexpected turn of events plunges characters into a stupor ('une émotion qui avait arrêté toutes mes pensées', 'cet étonnement qui laisse l'âme comme morte') which indicates that they respond to deeper calls than those which we can hear. They frequently understand more than they are able to express ('ce que je dis-là, je le sentais par instinct', 'on devine mieux ces choses-là qu'on ne les explique') for their understanding is even subtler than the tongue of Marianne. Beneath their faces, beneath their actions and their words lies a unifying internal reality — and it was with this richer inner life that Marivaux was ultimately concerned.

## 3 *Hearts and heads*

Marivaux's analysis of human nature is sophisticated and profound, but its range is narrow. He does not concern himself with the torments of love and jealousy nor with extremes of despair and evil (though Mme de Sainte-Hermières and her protégé, the *abbé*, are among his cruellest inventions). He was interested in the more intimate and comparatively unexciting affectations and failings of characters who exist in a sharply-defined present. He describes Tervire's upbringing and equips both Marianne and Jacob with sturdy provincial values, but he dismisses their early years and the formative influence of childhood as dull and unimportant. Thirty years before Rousseau made children interesting, Marivaux hurries his offspring towards adulthood with indecent haste: Marianne does not linger over the misfortune which robbed her of her parents because 'ce n'est pas y être que de l'éprouver à l'âge de deux ans' (*4*, 52). We are told little about how Jacob and Marianne came to be what they are, but their lack of background and context does not make them two-dimensional. Marivaux delivers them complete and fully formed. Although they aspire to progress, their true vocation is stasis, the endless unravelling of their own natures. The further they advance, the slower time passes. Jacob's adventures, if we exclude the four months spent as a valet, occupy no more than two weeks, and Desfontaines, one of Marivaux's bitterest critics, rightly pointed out that Marianne's readers would be dead before she ended her story. Marivaux does not offer complete lives for our inspection but total glimpses of brief moments: past and future yield to a brightly lit now.

There is movement, however. The skittish Marianne of the 'belles hardes' period turns into a mature observer of human affairs and Jacob shakes off his picaresque skin to reveal a more dignified 'honnête homme'. And if we see them change and develop, their 'metamorphosis' (to use Jacob's word) is presided over by their older, wiser selves who look on with amused and frequently ironical tolerance. What they are is also presented in terms of what they were and from this dual perspective (which Jean Rousset has called Marivaux's 'double registre') stems much of the depth which informs the pursuit of their inner reality. It is the narrators who explain what they had only intuitively felt. 'Tout ce que je vous dis là, je ne l'aurais point exprimé, mais je le sentais' (*4*, 74), says the older Marianne who adds: 'Je ne vois mes fautes que lorsque je les ai faites; c'est le moyen de les voir sûrement' (*4*, 89). If she is 'incorrigibly' prone to her 'reflections', which are so many commentaries on herself in particular and on human nature in general, Jacob the memorialist is similarly impelled by 'un esprit de réflexion' which he directs onto 'les événements de ma vie ' (*6*, 25-6). By interchanging the now of the narration with the now of events, Marivaux enables his narrators to double as explicators who turn their particular experience into general truths. For they are intermediaries between their past and the reader whom they claim to resemble: 'je suis ce que vous voyez, ce que vous êtes peut-être', Marianne tells her fictitious correspondent, 'ce qu'en général nous sommes tous' (*4*, 291). It is a clear invitation from Marivaux to judge his characters — but in the knowledge that our judgment may at any time be turned against ourselves.

Even the stray remarks of Marivaux's characters reinforce the mystery of motives which spring inevitably from affective urges. Jacob notes that Mlle Habert is torn 'entre le souci de me voir si aimé et la satisfaction de me voir si aimable' (*6*, 91) and further observes that there are people, like Agathe, 'qui aiment mieux leurs amis dans la douleur que dans la joie' (*6*, 116). Even he places greater trust in his feelings — 'le sentiment me menait ainsi, et il me menait bien' (*6*, 96) — than in his ready wit, and like Marianne he trusts implicitly in his sensitivity to tones of voice, facial expressions and gestures. She however, has a more complex affective system which on occasions becomes overloaded: each new situation propels her into 'un pays étranger' and she needs a moment to 'me concentrer' (*4*, 166). Whereas Jacob is merely left at a loss for words — for example when his marriage is interrupted by M. Doucin — Marianne is deprived of speech and thought: 'les personnes qui ont du sentiment sont bien plus abattues que d'autres dans de certaines occasions, parce que tout ce qui leur arrive les pénètre; il y a une tristesse stupide qui les prend' (*4*, 68). Such states of insensibility are frequently followed by a keener vision and Marianne's progress towards self-awareness is regularly punctuated by such shocks and flashes of insight. She does not, for instance, understand the implication of Climal's kindness (which 'm'étonnait sans rien m'apprendre' (*4*, 71)). She is vaguely uneasy, however: 'je rougissais sans savoir pourquoi, seulement par un instinct qui me mettait en peine de ce que cela pouvait signifier' (*4*, 67). Yet though her vanity tempts her to deceive herself, 'je vis dans ses yeux quelque chose de si ardent, que ce fut un coup de foudre pour moi' (*4*, 72). Her instincts are therefore true but they are buried deep, just as Jacob's natural impulses are overlaid by the prospect of getting his hands on Geneviève's money. The Marianne and the Jacob who write their stories are in command of the instinct which motivated their younger selves. The only difference is that they are older and that their experience has taught them to know their own natures and to follow where their affective being beckons — sure in the knowledge that they will not be led astray. Their 'metamorphosis' consists in this passage from confused and unworthy desires towards a state of conscious identity in which instincts and impulses have been cleansed not simply of moral baseness but of anything which demeans their self-regard. Their progress hinges less on money and social advancement than on the need to live in harmony with what they sense they are. It is in this light that we are to understand their ambition to 'parvenir'. When their motives cease to be ambiguious to themselves — and only then —, feeling, being and doing will coincide exactly. Only then will they have the simple directness of Mme de Miran who cuts through Marianne's tearful confusion with her 'Est-ce qu'il ne t'aime plus?' (*4*, 365).

Marivaux's insistence on the primacy of feeling takes him perilously close to outright sentimentality, and nowhere more so than in *Marianne*, which is awash with tears of surprise, joy, sadness, sympathy and dismay. Jacob is not immune to such effusions — 'je lui rendis les larmes qu'elle versait pour moi; elle en pleura encore davantage pour me récompenser de ce que je pleurais. . .' (*6*, 115) — but his more positive character does not require him to be as affected so deeply. Although these tears may sometimes be shed for effect, Marivaux clearly intended them as a form of sincerity. The capacity to weep spontaneously for oneself and for others is a direct expression, untouched by reason or vanity, of a certain nobility of heart. Though we may share a passing sympathy for the *spectre*'s dislike of such 'vertus romanesques' (*4*, 305), Marivaux's occasional excesses do not disguise the very high value he placed on a 'bon cœur' which is preferable to the 'belle âme' which has obligations to itself 'qui s'entêtent trop de la gloire ou de plaisir d'être généreux' (*4*, 171).

By a 'good heart', the ultimate test by which Marianne judges herself and others, Marivaux meant a constitutional affability, a natural and permanent concern for the feelings and welfare of our fellows. It makes no demands on those it serves and asks for no return. When it is 'tendre', 'généreux', 'franc' and 'honnête', it is admirable in a way that no other of our faculties can match. It is the seat of virtue. It allows us to live in peace with ourselves and is the only lasting source of consolation. Duty is no part of it and honesty and sincerity are not enough. Unless our feelings are actively aroused – by sympathy, compassion or love – our kindness will be short-lived and our charity empty.

Marianne readily acknowledges that the heart itself has desires which must be resisted – selfish desires which stem from the indulgence of pride. But if she recognises that pride is insidious, she is also aware that it is complex and is careful not to reject it out of hand on moral or religious grounds. Instead, she makes a number of fine distinctions which reveal the limits within which pride may be tolerated in a good and virtuous heart. 'La gloire' is indistinguishable from arrogance, and 'l'orgueil' makes us complacent towards ourselves and intolerant of others. 'Vanity', though it takes in all of Marianne's categories, is less easy to dismiss out of hand for while it may enlarge the opinion we have of ourselves, it also helps us to resist the false opinion which other people may hold of us. A degree of vanity protects us from ourselves and from those around us: it is the basis of self-respect and permits us to have confidence in our judgments and our qualities. Marianne worries a great deal, for instance, about her coquetry ('un enfant de l'orgueil' (*4*, 88)) lest it corrupt her entirely. Yet she is sufficiently objective to realise that the prospect of finding true love recedes 'quand la vanité d'en inspirer nous quitte' (*4*, 114): coquetry is redeemed by 'la pudeur'. Even so, she denounces the vanity of sacred orators (*4*, 199), of the 'préjugés vulgaires' enshrined in certain literary *salons* (*4*, 215), and even of the reader who is too delicate to follow the adventures of a mere 'lingère' (*4*, 87). She goes to great lengths to demonstrate the destructive and isolating effects of vanity in hearts which are more 'susceptible' than firm: 'ne savez-vous pas que notre âme est encore plus superbe que vertueuse, plus glorieuse qu'honnête, et par conséquent plus délicate sur les intérêts de sa vanité que sur ceux de son véritable honneur?' (*4*, 97). The desire to appear better than we are is the greatest single source of social and personal unhappiness.

Yet Marianne also concedes that 'chacun a son petit orgueil' (*4*, 307), and regards a measure of pride as natural and desirable. La Rochefoucauld had denounced 'amour-propre' as the begetter of all human folly and on the whole Marianne is inclined to agree. But she frequently uses his word in a more favourable sense: she thinks little of the act of charity which humiliates the 'amour-propre' of the recipient (*4*, 66), while Tervire's mother, more fortunate than Marianne had been, is able to accept an offer of money with an 'honnête et généreuse fierté' (*4*, 486). Though 'fierté' seems on occasion to be closely related to both 'gloire' and 'orgueil', Marianne recommends a certain 'fierté de cœur' (*4*, 105) both as a defence against others and as a source of moral consistency. The 'sentiment de fierté' (*4*, 342) is a form of self-esteem which defines our personality for us and enable us to distinguish not only between good and evil but also between what is vulgar and what is honourable. To act against our 'fierté' is to invite unease; to behave in accordance with it is to achieve the self-respect which brings a full measure of self-contentment (*4*, 178, 495).

Jacob is a much less subtle analyst of his vanity, but he reaches similar conclusions. He allows us to see him swept up into 'un tourbillon de vanité flatteuse' as he delights in his new name, his new clothes and the unaccustomed attentions of his betters. Yet he is quite aware that 'la vanité de plaire' leads him into 'de lâches complaisances' (*6*, 131) and he pours scorn on those weak enough to apologise for their humble birth: 'une fierté sensée' is to be preferred to such 'orgueil impertinent' (*6*, 25). Like Marianne, he has a quick eye for pride in others, for his awareness of his own vanity enables him to detect sham and conceit 'même sans y penser' (*6*, 187). But though he readily draws our attention to his pride, he insists upon its role in shaping the charity and consideration which he so admires: it is 'une vanité qui me rendait gai, et non pas superbe et ridicule; mon amour-propre a toujours été sociable; je n'ai jamais été plus doux ni plus traitable que lorsque j'ai eu lieu de m'estimer et d'être vain; chacun a là-dessus son caractère, et c'était là le mien' (6, 174-5). If he tries to appear more sophisticated and more attractive than he is, it is in good measure because he seeks to please and not because he wishes to impose himself on others for base and self-interested motives. Jacob is thus not vain, but 'fier'.

Vanity nevertheless regularly threatens to undermine true good-ness and it is well served by reason. Reason may appear to contri-bute a welcome dose of objectivity to problems of conduct, for its accepted role in moral matters is to call the heart to order. Yet even Jacob knows that it is dangerous since it encourages us to commit actions which we secretly know to be wrong. Mlle Habert, pressed by her sister and M. Doucin to send Joseph away but also pressurised by her heart to keep him, resorts to moral reasons (her debt of grati-tude to her rescuer) to justify what her passion demands. Reason may deceive us as completely as vanity does, and Jacob reinforces his point by showing us a number of *dévotes* who convince them-selves that they would be wrong to desire what they cannot in any case have. But though he might suggest that reason brings neither consolation nor self-contentment, his own behaviour seems fre-quently to be dictated more by conscious self-interest than by an open and honest heart. He allows cupidity to debate with his honour, but finds that honour 'a besoin de parler longtemps, lui, pour faire impression, et qu'il a plus de peine à persuader que les passions' (6, 42). But in fact, the quarrel within him is not waged between reason and feeling but between contrary pulls of his sensibility: honour is an adjunct of 'fierté' and not an intellectual concept. Though he seems to make a career of running after women, he always feels something for them: the only calculation that enters into his love affairs is his difficulty in distinguishing between what is mere sensuality and what is true sensibility. The sole regulator of conduct is therefore not 'la raison' but a well-constituted 'cœur'. D'Orville's love for his wife is complacent and lacking in 'tendresse' and it denies him 'une certaine finesse de sentiment, et lui épaissit extrêmement l'intelligence' (6, 231). But when properly tender and 'fier', feeling generates its own lucidity and makes reason redundant. It is by this yardstick that we must judge Mme de Fécour who is more sensual than sensitive, or the good Mme d'Alain whose natural goodness lacks both guile and discretion. 'Les âmes excessivement bonnes sont volontiers imprudentes par excès de bonté même, et d'un autre côté, les âmes prudentes sont assez rarement bonnes' (*6*, 102). If love has its 'métaphysique', then feeling has its rationale.

As we might expect, Marianne takes Jacob's 'finesse de sentiment' and defines it in greater detail. Like him, she suspects anyone whose heart is not controlled by that self-esteem which makes us aware of what we owe to ourselves and to others. Mme Dutour may be fundamentally good-hearted but her feelings are unregulated and, like Mme d'Alain, her indiscretion may do as much harm as the malice of Mme de Fare. Valville's heart is immature for, being no more than 'susceptible' it lacks consistency (*4*, 336). Marianne has a theoretical respect for rational thinking, but in practice she observes that reason is frequently misused — even by philosophers who rate knowledge above good sense and who rarely display that insight in which 'la vérité leur échappe d'abondance de cœur' (*4*, 60). For most people, the age of reason is 'bien plutôt l'âge de la folie' (*4*, 59) and Marianne is very wary of 'l'art impeccable de mes petits raisonnements' (*4*, 145). She concludes from her experience that 'il n'y a que le sentiment qui nous puisse donner des nouvelles un peu sûres de nous, et qu'il ne faut pas trop se fier à celles que notre esprit veut faire à sa guise, car je le crois un grand visionnaire' (*4*, 60). Mme de Miran is more prepared to tolerate a 'cœur faible' than 'un esprit impertinent et corrompu' (*4*, 173), and if Marianne has a reservation about her it is precisely that 'son esprit bornait la bonté de son cœur' (*4*, 212). Yet it is in Mme de Miran that we find 'le sentiment d'un cœur excellent' which makes her kind without indulgence and lucid without asperity. She has 'cette bonté proprement dite qui tiendrait lieu de lumière, même aux personnes qui n'auraient pas d'esprit, et qui, parce qu'elle est vraie bonté, veut avec scrupule être juste et raisonnable' (*4*, 171). Our conduct can never be superior to our feelings, which condition what we desire and what we do. A good heart disciplined by a measure of 'fierté' will defend us against the tricks of reason and pride, for from 'la finesse des sentiments' itself will emerge a less destructive form of self-awareness which will lead us instinctively to what is 'juste et raisonnable'.

The role which Marivaux accords to sensibility reveals him in an anti-intellectual stance which sets him apart from the rational thrust of his century. Yet he was sufficiently a man of his time to wish to communicate his concept of the intelligent heart as a sure means of combatting the egoism which is the permanent obstacle to personal and collective happiness. Yet he seems to imply that 'un bon cœur' is a natural asset rather than something we can learn: 'ce n'est que par accident que nous vivons, mais c'est naturellement que nous sommes' (*4*, 142). Villot, Marianne's graceless suitor, seems beyond recovery since he is a weak man 'à qui il n'appartenait pas d'avoir du cœur' (*4*, 300). On the other hand, Marivaux does suggest, in one of the rare comments he makes about education, that had Tervire's mother not neglected 'de régler le cœur et l'esprit' of her son, his vanity would not have got the better of him (*4*, 494). But if Jacob, Marianne and Tervire appear to belong to an élite of right-feeling individuals licensed for goodness by nature and not by their education, they were clearly intended to be seen as part of common humanity. In 1719, Marivaux had noted that we are all capable of love or hate or perfidy and are 'susceptibles de sentiments vicieux, lâches et vertueux, suivant la nature des impressions qui [nous] frappent le plus dans l'occasion' (*2*, 67). In 1748, in the *Réflexions sur l'esprit humain*, he was still writing that 'toutes les âmes ont une ressemblance générale: il y a de tout dans chacune d'elles, nous avons tous les commencements de ce qui nous manque' (*2*, 472). Tervire thus seems to point the way ahead when she says of 'le cœur humain' that 'chacun a d'abord le sien, et puis un peu de celui de tout le monde' (*4*, 412). The world of Marivaux's novels may sometimes have a pessimistic tinge: for every Mme de Miran there are many immoral and self-seeking men and women. Yet without ever quite preaching human perfectibility (an abstract notion foreign to his way of thinking), Marivaux does suggest that though we may not all respond to teaching, then at least the ideal of 'le cœur fier' may be revealed to us. It may be revealed by example — Mme de Miran is a source of inspiration to Marianne — but it is best and most permanently divulged through love.

Of all the bonds that draw individuals together, only love has the power to steer us towards virtue. Stronger than affection, gratitude, compassion or even friendship, true love is the surest road to self-knowledge. Marivaux warns us to beware of imitations. Marianne's 'officier' loves with his head – 'c'est ma raison qui vous a donné mon cœur, je n'ai pas apporté ici d'autre passion' (*4*, 374) – and though the 'estime' and 'amitié' he offers are admirable in their way, they are limited and earthbound. Physical attraction may seem to supply the missing poetic dimension, but proves to be even less satisfactory. Valville is drawn to Marianne by the sight of her pretty ankle, but the love he feels for her is cancelled by a glimpse of Varthon's 'corps délacé'. Like M. de Climal or the *abbé* who seduces Tervire's unfortunate friend, Valville is too sensual to be the ideal 'amant délicat' in whom 'les sentiments du cœur se mêlent avec les sens' (*4*, 75). Valville turns out to be the inconstant lover whose self-love is satisfied by conquest. If he appears to illustrate La Rochefoucauld's view of love as an expression of our 'amour-propre', and if Marivaux's analysis of love ('égards', 'délicatesse', 'estime', 'tendresse', etc.) seems to look back to the categories devised by seventeenth-century 'précieuses', we should not conclude that *Marianne* and *Le Paysan* simply revive the notion of the harmony of twin souls.

Marivaux's lovers love at first sight, but the earth does not tremble nor are they overtaken by a 'coup de foudre'. Love is a stealthy thing which creeps up on them, taking them unawares and identifying itself only as an afterthought. When Marianne first sees Valville, she is aware of strange feelings to which she cannot give a name: she leaves the church 'avec un cœur à qui il manquait quelque chose, et qui ne savait pas ce que c'était' (*4*, 92). She experiences a 'trouble des sens' and vague 'mouvements inconnus' which she does not understand until much later: 'j'ai pris d'abord de l'inclination pour lui, tout d'abord sans savoir que c'était de l'amour, je n'y songeais pas; j'avais seulement du plaisir à le voir, je le trouvais estimable' (*4*, 186). But even before she is aware of her true feelings, love sharpens her insight and drives her away from vanity towards a 'sentiment de fierté' – still unconsciously, and on the profoundest affective level where sensibility maximises the 'esprit' of the good heart. She ceases to be a coquette and sees through Climal and her foolish pride. Love works on her instincts and with the dawning of love she is impelled permanently towards the goodness and honour which will become the poles of her conscious personality.

Jacob, more sensual by nature than Marianne, is no less permanently transformed by love. With Mlle Habert, his protestations go
from the 'plaisant' and the 'obligeant' to the 'flatteur' and the
'tendre'. But what he feels for her is not true love but merely a
sincere regrard: 'ce n'était que par instinct que j'en agissais ainsi, et
l'instinct ne débrouille rien' (*6*, 79). He is well aware of the empti-
ness of those 'amours où le cœur n'a point de part' (*6*, 211) and
classes his adventures with Mme de Ferval and Mme de Fécour as
purely sensual. On the other hand, his meeting with Mme D'Orville
is momentous. In his eyes, she has 'un charme secret', 'mais je ne
croyais que l'estimer, la plaindre et m'intéresser à ce qui la regar-
dait; . . . pour amour ni d'aucun sentiment approchant, il n'en était
pas question dans mon esprit' (*6*, 192). Mme D'Orville is similarly
affected: she blushes 'sans qu'elle-même sût pourquoi' (*6*, 193).
Though Jacob's story stops short of his discovery of what he feels
for her, it is clear that his subconscious attraction to her hastens his
progress towards the honour and 'fierté' which mark him out as one
of Marivaux's elect. He ceases to be a *pícaro* as Marianne ceases to be
a coquette.Though he loves Mme D'Orville 'sans le savoir encore'
(*6*, 231), Jacob's hitherto undirected, natural impulses begin to turn
into a sense of honour and that intuitive understanding which characterises the interventions of Jacob the narrator. Like Marianne (and
for that matter Tervire who also goes through the 'surprise de
l'amour' which features so often in Marivaux's plays), he is on the
way to gaining control of his instincts through love.

Marivaux's interest in the inner life provides the common de-
nominator for those complexities and contradictions which both
Jacob and Marianne once found difficult to express: the world they
show us is filtered through that sensibility which slowly reveals itself
to them. If they are complex and prone to error, their judgments are
unified by an intuitive perception which, if not always conscious, is
always consistent. This insistence on their internal reality may not
stem from any overt moral or social purpose on Marivaux's part, but
it clearly has implications both for the individual and for society.
Marianne and Jacob are far more satisfactory as human and social
beings than the many vain, selfish and hypocritical churchmen,
ladies of fashion and pillars of the community with whom they have

to deal. Natural virtue does exist — in the country priest and his sister who give Marianne a home, or in the good farmers who raised Jacob and Tervire — but it is scarce, and admired more than it is practised. Society sets a higher value on success than on goodness ('c'est assez là le chemin des honneurs: qui les mérite n'y arrive guère' (*4*, 110) and shows more respect for the haughty 'belle âme' than for the simple 'bon cœur': 'il faut que la terre soit un séjour bien étranger pour la vertu, car elle ne fait qu'y souffrir' (*4*, 57). It is of course paradoxical that neither Marianne nor Jacob aspire to this naïve and unsophisticated form of virtue. However much we try to explain their embattled goodness, it is not easy to explain it away. They lack charity towards their enemies and are impatient with fools (that is, with defective sensibilities). In the defence of their 'bons cœurs', they exhibit a steely sense of purpose and in pursuit of their self-interest show a deviousness at which Marivaux himself connives. Jacob is more likeable for his faults than for his successes, while Marianne never ceases to be slightly forbidding. Before we can accept them as 'parvenus' in more than the social sense, we must first accept their values.

# 4 *Values*

Marianne's practice of virtue is never quite without an air of calculation: if she blooms when love and kindness shine on her, it is difficult to avoid the thought that there is a worm in the bud. Jacob's
successes depend more obviously still on a talent for justifying
dubious actions: he may rise naturally, like bread, but the result is
not entirely wholesome. What is equally puzzling is that Marivaux
plots with them and visibly intervenes to ensure that they reap the
rewards due to their 'bon cœur'. Unlike the unfortunate Tervire,
Marianne does not lose by her preference for truth and honour,
while the quite genuine humanitarianism which prompts Jacob to
help Mlle Habert, decline D'Orville's sinecure and rescue Dorsan,
is not allowed to go without tangible recompenses, for it is the
source of his fortune and, we may surmise, of his love. Marivaux
here seems rather more than simply over-protective. He appears to
underwrite opportunism and the most insidious kind of moral
duplicity.

Part of the problem lies in the fact that both novels assume an
ethical principle which no longer commands general sympathy. Since
about the time of the Romantics, we have grown accustomed to
judging actions by their consequences. Theologically, sin is still defined in terms of 'l'advertance' which implies the existence of a
degree of deliberate intent, but in the context of both morality and
law, good intentions have ceased to be an adequate defence. Like
many of his contemporaries, Marivaux subscribed to the view that
moral blame cannot attach to actions whose consequences are as
unforseen as they are unpremeditated. It is such a theory of intention which helps to explain why Prévost felt able to absolve Des
Grieux who cannot be guilty of a murder he never intended to
commit. Mme d'Alain and Mme Dutour may be good-hearted but
they are guilty of avoidable indiscretion, for though the consequences of their actions are not premeditated they are foreseeable.
But Marianne's virtuous instincts and Jacob's honorable impulses
rule out the possibility that they knowingly seek to translate good

actions into material advantages. And if they intend no evil, they cannot be accused of using virtue to secure the benefits which Marivaux offers them. They may be ready enough to profit from the favourable consequences of their actions, but their motives are beyond reproach. Marivaux many times stresses their fundamental innocence. It is 'avec une innocence d'intention admirable' (*6*, 192) rather than with any thought of trading on his good deed that Jacob dines with Mme D'Orville. And if Marianne admits that she wears her 'belles hardes' for longer than decency permits, 'c'était par un petit raisonnement que mes besoins et ma vanité m'avaient dicté, et qui n'avait rien pris sur la pureté de mes intentions' (*4*, 79). They set out to deceive no one, least of all themselves. Their behaviour is therefore as blameless as their motives. To both motive and conduct they apply a simple but infallible test which has little to do with the principles of religion or morality: good actions are those which allow them to feel at ease with themselves, while unworthy actions immediately make them feel uncomfortable. If they are expert in sensing (rather than in deducing) fraud in others, it is because they have disciplined their sensibility, which not only replaces reason but also takes over the functions of conscience. Jacob's sense of honour and Tervire's need to feel 'honnête pour soi' (*4*, 500) which Marianne shares, are in the first instance more a matter of sensation than of analysis. And when they feel at ease with their sensibility, they are beyond reproach.

Marivaux's whole system of values is rooted more in feeling than in rational principles. His approach to religious, moral and social matters is determined not by ideas but by the conviction that exemplary conduct is an 'effet du cœur'. Jacob exposes the hypocrisy of directors of conscience and the bigotry of the *dévote*, but he hastens to add that the counsel provided by M. Doucin is 'louable et saint en lui-même' (*6*, 68) and that the 'truly pious' are exempt from his strictures (*6*, 123). Marianne may point out that sacred orators are vain men, but she reveres the country priest who raised her and describes Père Vincent as a 'bon religieux'. Clearly, Marivaux's anticlericalism was neither very deep nor very strong. Though *Marianne* takes us inside a number of convents, none is as destructive of freedom and personality as those which Diderot was to condemn in *La Religieuse*, nor does Marivaux go as far as to show

us a nun who has been demoralised by the cloistered life. He criti-
cises neither the corruption of the church nor the dishonesty of its
servants on any save the personal level. Nor does he appear to be
anything other than respectful towards a faith which he himself held
in moderate esteem. Jacob has more superstition than Christianity
in him: as a *pícaro*, he is much given to invoking the devil and when
in difficulties he prays 'même plus qu'à l'ordinaire, car on aime tant
Dieu, quand on a besoin de lui!' (*6*, 118). He shows how M. Doucin
was prepared to persecute him; how religion repressed the natural
sensuality of Mlle Habert who in marriage is greatly relieved 'de
pouvoir sans péché être aussi aise que les pécheurs' (*6*, 176); how
even the love of God had failed to settle the perpetual arguments
which divide the Habert sisters (*6*, 74-5). Jacob's reservations attack
the puritanical spirit of narrow observance and the use of religion as
a prop for the inadequate or tool of the unscrupulous: he nowhere
suggests that faith is not commendable. In *Marianne*, Marivaux
expresses rather more positive sentiments. There is no reason to suspect him of insincerity when he suggests, for example, that Tervire's
mother is punished by Providence. Like M. de Climal, who dies in an
odour of sanctity, Mme de Sainte-Hermières also returns to God who
'[lui] fit la grâce de la punir pour la sauver' (*4*, 421-2).

In *Le Cabinet du Philosophe* (*2*, 364), Marivaux argues that
justice, like all social and moral values, derives from God alone. Man
'n'était fait que pour avoir un maître, qui était Dieu; et le péché lui
en a donné mille'. Marivaux's faith does not shine like a beacon, but
he did believe that though virtue was the work of the heart, it was
underwritten by heaven. His view is nowhere more clearly expressed
than in his discussion of charity. In both novels, charity is used to
disguise base motives, to acquire social reputation and to increase
self-esteem. Jacob consistently denounces the ostensibly charitable
motives of pious ladies who merely want to get their hands on him,
but it is Marianne, regularly humiliated by the self-directed kindness
of others, who argues the fuller case against what she describes as an
'œuvre de métier et non de sentiment' (*4*, 66). The true charity
shown by Mme de Miran, Tervire and even M. Bono, emerges not
only as a virtue of the heart but as a Christian duty.

However, Marivaux's acknowledgement of religious values is
vague and sometimes eccentric. He took no philosophical interest in

the question of God's existence nor does he set Him up as the fount of conscience. His theological and moral views often seem under-considered and even unorthodox. Jacob might call his master's tempting proposition 'la pomme d'Adam revenue pour moi' (*6*, 42), but Marivaux had no wish to depict the world in terms of dogma. There is far more human vice than sin in his characters and if Marianne noted that 'il faut bien parler du Destin' (*4*, 56), there is little to suggest that the destiny which directs her and Jacob is the will of God. The evil-intentioned, like M. de Climal, or the innocent-ly self-deluding, like Mlle Habert, are always ready to talk of Provi-dence and Tervire even invokes 'la grâce'. But for the most part, Jacob and Marianne speak of 'le sort', 'le hasard', 'mon étoile', 'une espèce de fatalité', 'l'accident' or simply 'l'inconstance des choses de ce monde'. Jacob is not unduly worried by his conclusion that 'il n'y a que chance dans ce monde' (*6*, 29), and Marianne shares his general view that though fate is a force to be reckoned with, it is not always hostile. Both confront their destiny with optimism, for they are not only resilient but pragmatic. 'Les petits arrangements qu'on prend d'avance sont assez souvent inutiles', says Marianne with a shrug; 'c'est la manière dont les choses tournent qui décide de ce qu'on dit ou de ce qu'on fait en pareilles occasions; mais ces sortes de prépar-ations vous amusent et vous soulagent' (*4*, 278). If Marivaux here seems to express sentiments which are not merely anti-rationalist but anti-Christian, it was because he saw life as a human and not a cosmic drama. The chance which allows Marianne to be run down by a cab or to meet Mme de Miran is the same chance that enables Jacob to help Mlle Habert and save Dorsan. As events, they are sig-nificant only because Marianne and Jacob are equipped to make the most of their opportunities.

Marivaux thus adopts a highly personal view of Providence and, more curious still, expresses idiosyncratic attitudes to a range of moral and social issues. He says nothing very constructive about marriage nor does he raise associated issues such as adultery or the dowry system. His conception of love scarcely seems a satisfactory basis for marriage if we are to conclude that for every Marianne there are many Valvilles and Dursans who misread their own hearts. Jacob's mistress has an empty fashionable marriage, while the anec-dote told by the 'officier' who travels in the coach to Versailles

(*6*, 177ff.) paints a squalid picture of conjugal conflict. M. Dursan and Brunon hardly recommend the institution and Tervire's brother is scarcely an ideal husband to his selfish wife. Even the sweet Mme D'Orville has married the wrong man. Nor is there more to be said for family life than for marriage. Indeed, Marianne should think herself lucky if Marivaux intend as norms the problems Mme de Miran has with Valville, Dursan's quarrel with his mother or the bickering of the Habert sisters. Perhaps we should not be suprised that their marriages fail and their family life is disrupted, for Marivaux clearly found most of his characters objectionable in varying degrees. Apart from one or two saintly figures, the men are weak or fickle or depraved and the women deceitful, envious and malicious.

But we should not conclude that Marivaux was a devout misanthropist, for his criticisms are tempered not only by good humour but by paradox. Thus if he seems to accuse women of surrendering to the 'minauderies' of their sex, to the feminine weaknesses of idle curiosity, foolish vanity and gossip ('toute femme a du caquet', notes Jacob (*6*, 84)), it is nevertheless clear that he genuinely admires their cast of mind. Women 'ont le jugement sûr' (*4*, 170) when they deal with other women, while they decipher the looks men give them with great delicacy: 'ce sont de ces choses qui ne nous échappent point' (*4*, 286). Though nothing may be said for the woman who is merely vain, Marivaux not only justified coquetry as natural but as an additional source of that sensibility in which all our ideas are located. As a woman, Marianne claims to have two sorts of 'esprit', that which nature has given her and that which 'la vanité de plaire nous donne' (*4*, 88). What she lacks in bookish learning or worldly experience is amply compensated by her 'instinct de femme'. Although Jacob does not have her advantages — 'nous autres jolies femmes... personne n'a plus d'esprit que nous quand nous en avons un peu' (*4*, 50) — it is clear that within his masculine body there lurks a somewhat feminine sensibility which gives him a comparable insight into other people's motives, a temperamental compassion and that vulnerability which redeems his aggression. Marivaux's moral values originate, in the last analysis, not from general principles but from a concept of sensibility which he normally associates with women.[3]

[3]  Though the 'sentimental revolution' is frequently identified with the pub-

Of course, he recommends honesty, generosity and true charity as clearly as he denounces the greed, pride and self-interest which motivates human behaviour at all social levels — from the valet who robs Jacob's master to Mme Rémy who lives on immoral earnings and the Brunons and Climals who use their money to oppress the innocent. Yet Marivaux also approves of actions and attitudes which depart from the common ethical norms. Jacob's mistress leads a patently immoral life, but because she lives it without 'vanité' or 'gloire' and 'comme on vivrait dans l'état le plus décent et le plus ordinaire' (*6*, 28-9), she is the moral superior of Marianne's abbess or the 'respectable' Mme de Ferval. M. Bono's bluntness may seem incompatible with conventional notions of kindness, but there is no doubting his humane concern. Marianne and Jacob are only too well aware that conventional morality is for most people a kind of sanitised hypocrisy, and accordingly their conduct is intended to be truly good, and not merely to appear so. As though to excuse the more ambiguous of his actions, Jacob admits that 'on fait comme on peut, on n'est ni des saints ni des saintes' (*6*, 165). But though they might err, it was enough for Marivaux that his protagonists should follow the promptings of instinct and the impulses of an intelligent heart.

He was not, however, so idealistic as to imagine that it was enough simply to establish them as honest practitioners of 'la science du cœur'. Their 'aristocratic' hearts were no guarantee of the social position to which their affective virtue entitles them. Like many others before and since, Marivaux observed that wealth and power are given to the hard of heart while honest men stay poor and helpless: 'Que peuvent devenir les malheureux qui par là n'ont de ressource dans l'abondance des uns ni dans la compassion des autres?' (*2*, 129). Jacob is very conscious of this paradox which Marivaux had explored in greater detail in *L'Île des Esclaves* (1725). His master's veiled threat teaches him that 'l'on met au cachot les personnes qui ont de l'honneur, et en chambre garnie celles qui n'en

lication of Rousseau's novel, *La Nouvelle Héloïse*, in 1761, a mood of reaction against a purely rational perception of the world is noticeable much earlier in the century — in the novels of Prévost, for example, or the *théâtre larmoyant* of La Chaussée. Sensibility was defended not only as an expression of true personality but also as the basis of moral action and religious belief. Against the 'philosophic' insistence on reason, the man and woman of feeling urged the primacy of the emotions. As rationalism declined, it was this concept of sensibility which was to form the core of the new Romantic ideal.

ont point' (*6*, 46) and, observing his mistress deserted by her friends, he reflects that 'dans ce monde, toutes les vertus sont déplacées, aussi bien que les vices. Les bons et les mauvais cœurs ne se trouvent point à leur place' (*6*, 51). Even Marianne is led to speculate that if titles were given to those who deserved them, 'qu'il y aurait de madames ou de mademoiselles qui ne seraient plus que des Manons et des Cathos!' (*4*, 298). Jacob and Marianne deserve to succeed precisely because they understand that money and privilege, far from being ends in themselves, carry the responsibility of charity which their 'cœur tendre et raisonnable' eminently fits them to discharge.

Marivaux was not tempted to see the problem in political terms — Jacob's protest, when summoned before the magistrate having done no wrong, that he is a victim of arbitrary power, strikes a rare note — nor even in terms of class. On the whole, he shared the view expressed by the 'supérieure' of the convent where Marianne is forcibly held, that 'la différence des conditions est une chose nécessaire dans la vie' (*4*, 273). He also seems to have agreed with Mlle Habert that while all men are equal in the sight of God, proper respect is due 'aux coûtumes établies parmi nous' (*6*, 125). The rich are the guiltiest for their responsibilities are the greatest. But Marivaux held no brief for the populace who are stupid and easily led. The 'canaille' merely gape as Mme Dutour confronts the coachman or Dorsan fights for his life. Jacob may be proud of his country stock, yet his own brother proves to be a snob and the Habert sisters have none of the virtues of their heredity. Servants serve unwillingly, resentful of their servitude (*4*, 217), and their masters despise their pursuit of 'de quoi vivre, et de quoi se retirer de la bassesse de leur condition' (*6*, 44). As we ascend the social scale (which is much wider in the memoirs of Jacob who rises by degrees, whereas Marianne positively leaps from her shop-counter into the upper middle classes), we encounter no one who reflects credit or discredit on their class in general terms: they are admirable or despicable as individuals. Tradespeople like Mme Dutour, the grocer or Jacob's cobbler have limited minds but occasionally good hearts — Mme d'Alain, a lawyer's widow, for example. The churchmen and -women we encounter are contradictory as a group, while the ladies of quality and men of rank do not amount to a systematic critique of their caste. But all classes share one divisive characteristic: they envy their betters and despise their inferiors, a phenomenon which Jacob describes as neither very humble nor very Christian (*6*, 127-8). Even Mme Dorsin is appalled that Valville should condescend to dress as a servant in order to see Marianne (*4*, 183), though in her salon 'il n'était point question de rang ni d'états' (*4*, 215). Mme d'Alain is rude about the grocer who is 'marguiller de sa paroisse' (*6*, 114), though she adopts a wary egalitarianism towards Jacob in whom she sees a future 'maître' (*6*, 109). Mme de Fécour on the other hand treats rich and poor alike – but only because no one interests her sufficently to be treated in any distinctive way.

Neither Marianne nor Jacob attempt to conceal their origins, though, making a virtue of their misfortune, they adapt quickly to circumstances. Marianne's quality is soon established, but Jacob is no less successful in acquiring the 'mondanité' – far more important to him than mere money – which enables him to behave with growing assurance in prison, in a lady's boudoir, the halls of Versailles or the foyer of the Comédie Française. Neither is permanently impressed by rank, though both have a knack of detecting at a glance those who, wherever they are placed on the social scale (and they include Marianne's village priest, Mme de Miran, Mme Darneuil's maid, Jacob's mistress, Dorsan and M. Bono) are members of what might be called 'l'aristocratie du cœur'. It is in this light that they judge politicians, for instance: if Marianne's President is wily, his good heart justifies his paternalism (*4*, 288); if M. de Fécour has lost touch with social reality, it is because his heart is naturally hard (*6*, 191). They admit the notion of equality – 'les âmes ont-elles des parents?' asks the 'officier', 'ne sont-elles pas toutes d'une condition égale?' (*4*, 375) – but are prepared to extend it only to those who are clubbable. Jacob and Marianne could be excused of being heart-snobs if their moral being were not above reproach.

Marivaux was well aware that the acquisition of expensive habits is not without its dangers. Jacob never forgets how his brother was corrupted by his social advancement and observes that 'l'âme se raffine à mesure qu'elle se gâte' (*6*, 174). Yet though he passes from valet to bourgeois to 'honnête homme', his nature provides him with an immunity to corruption and Marivaux's occasional Rousseauistic reservations about the injurious effects of socialisation prove to be groundless. Tervire points out that 'il n'y a point de condition qui mette à l'abri du malheur' (*4*, 380) and it is equally true that no rank in society guarantees happiness. This is why Marivaux consistently rejects 'les usages et les maximes du monde' which deny Marianne the right to marry above her social position: her 'vraies richesses' are her beauty, 'bel esprit' and 'excellent cœur' (*4*, 184). Yet he had no wish to extend the courtesy to all and sundry. Mme Dursan might have consented to her son's marriage to Brunon had her origins been 'honnêtes' — Mlle Habert adopts similar criteria (*6*, 98-9) — but Brunon was 'une fille de la lie du peuple, et d'une famille connue pour l'infâme parmi le peuple' (*4*, 434). Events justify her opposition, but not on social grounds: Brunon is disqualified by her greed and cruelty. Clearly, there were limits to Marivaux's tolerance as there were to his egalitarianism, limits which were set by his evaluation of individuals and not by general notions of politics or class. 'On est tout d'un coup lié avec des gens qui ont le cœur bon, quels qu'ils soient', notes Tervire: 'ce sont comme des amis que vous avez dans tous les états' (*4*, 397). Ultimately, Marivaux's social hierarchy was based on a freemasonry of the heart.

Even so, he recognised that it is only in literature that virtue is rewarded. In real life, sinners prosper. Tervire's adventures, up to the moment when she berates her sister-in-law, demonstrate how consistently a trusting heart is abused by the unscrupulous. But how far may we go in protecting our virtue before we in turn cease to be virtuous? If goodness is worth having, then it is worth defending. But if our defensive strategy is tainted by deception or even excessive zeal, then we run the risk of undermining the moral integrity we seek to protect. Marivaux was inclined to state the perennial moral problem of ends and means in terms of the tension between bourgeois values and Christian ethics. In 1717, he had already shown that religion and business are incompatible. The merchant who trusts his competitors may save his soul but he will lose his money; the wealth of the man who trusts no one is earned at the expense of human kindness. However, 'il faut vivre et se sauver' and while, on balance, Marivaux acknowledged that the 'marchand' in us normally gets the better of our Christian selves, he believed that an accommodation was possible: 'il peut s'y trouver une bonne foi mitigée, qui, dégagée de la sévérité du précepte, s'accommode à l'avidité que les marchands ont de gagner sans voler absolument la religion' (*2*, 17). Marianne and Jacob may have righteous hearts, but they use market-place methods.

Indeed, they embody, in modified form, the economic individualism which Ian Watt detects in early eighteenth-century English fiction[4] and which makes *Robinson Crusoe*, for example, not merely an adventure story but a celebration of the spirit of mercantilism. Like Robinson, who is a very capitalist castaway, Jacob pauses to take stock of his material gains and Marianne's regular recapitulations of her progress reflect something of a balance-sheet mentality. Yet though they achieve the reward of merit, Marivaux's middle-class sympathies were far less positive than Defoe's. He was untouched by the more aggressive Protestant ethic and did not share the English admiration for commerce which, as Voltaire points out in the *Lettres philosophiques*, was at variance with the French social code. Addison and Steele had praised trade, which created wealth and spread knowledge; Marivaux, as 'le Spectateur français', readily denounces the crass materialism of the business ethic. As a good bourgeois, he speaks out against injustice, hypocrisy, ostentatious social climbers and arrogant aristocrats, and he approves of tender love, compassion, honesty, caring parents, dutiful children and upright public servants. But he stops short of bourgeois dynamism. Like Marianne, who regularly chides herself for being indolent, Marivaux several times confessed to being lazy and he had considerable reservations about ambition. He despised the greed of those who seek wealth and the pride of those who amass 'honneurs': the first are scoundrels and the second, though sometimes 'généreux', are 'méchants' and normally dangerous (*2*, 437). As Henri Coulet suggests (*8*, 59-71), Marivaux belongs not to the emerging 'bourgeoisie marchande et industrielle', but to the 'bourgeoisie financière' which set greater store by genteel consuming than by the spirit of enterprise. He may have earned his living by his pen, but he preferred the values of the gentleman.

It is not surprising therefore if Jacob and Marianne show more enthusiasm for having money than for getting it. However perilous their plight, they refuse to compromise for cash. Marianne resists Climal and Dutour who press her to sell her virtue, and she refuses to marry Villot who would at least have kept her in comfort. Most women who see Jacob urge him to 'faire fortune' by marrying for

[4] *The Rise of the Novel*, London, 1957.

money. But he marries Mlle Habert because he loves her after his fashion. If Marianne speaks of her 'fortune', she means 'celle de mon cœur', for she gives no thought 'aux biens de Valville, non plus qu'au rang qu'il me donnerait' (*4*, 259). Indeed, they openly scorn the pursuit of wealth. Marianne would rather overpay the coachman than be exposed to his vulgar abuse; Tervire is appalled by the change in Brunon who suddenly becomes rich; Jacob not only warns Geneviève against her master's money but tells her that 'quand vous en aurez jusqu'au cou, il faut en avoir par-dessus la tête' (*6*, 38). Yet their scorn for money has well-defined limits. Marianne has no financial worries after her adoption by Mme de Miran, whose charity she can accept because it is true. Jacob knows that 'le dernier des hommes ici-bas est celui qui n'a rien' (*6*, 44) and that his problem is that he has merit and no money (*6*, 29). He waxes almost hysterical at the sight of his new wealth and revels in his new clothes and property (*6*, 120, 157-8). Even M. Bono remarks that Mme D'Orville's romantic preference for handsome but impoverished nobles who kill wolves, is scarcely a practical attitude to life (*6*, 198). It is a lesson which does not have to be pointed out to Jacob and Marianne, whose passive opportunism is abetted by Marivaux at every turn. Marianne cannot be bought by Climal, but Marivaux enables her to take his money by turning him into a repentant sinner. She might worry about her 'belles hardes' but she goes on wearing them, and her vanity is rewarded since her pretty clothes help Valville to notice her and Mme de Miran to single her out. Nor can she be accused of pursuing Valville whom she leaves, out of decency, in ignorance of her address: honesty requires her to return Climal's presents and writing to Valville is the only method open to her — even though she is not without hope that her carefully composed letter may help him to trace her. Jacob reacts indignantly against M. Doucin, but proceeds to do what the Habert sisters were warned he might. If his sensuality threatens to subvert his honour, Marivaux rescues him by arranging for his tête-à-tête in Mme Rémy's house to be interrupted. At every turn, Marivaux intervenes not only to put the best possible interpretation upon their actions or to preserve their intentions intact, but to enable them to enjoy practical advantages which the real world would be less eager to offer them. If life seems to treat them exceptionally well, it is because Marivaux gives a bourgeois twist to their 'destiny', as he does also to love itself.

Traditionally, love was described in conventional images which reflected the place allotted to it in a well-regulated society. Metaphors of war and diplomacy ('victoire', 'attaquer un cœur', 'esclave') reduced passion to acceptable proportions while religious images ('idole', 'sacrifice', 'adorer') sanctified it. The contemporary novel drew upon these conventions as upon the growing number of expressions culled from economic affairs ('profiter', 'prix', 'coûter', 'commerce', etc.). Marivaux, however, shows less interest in religious and military imagery than in economic and business terms, as Frédéric Deloffre has shown (*10*, 257-60). Though this metaphorical theme is 'plus caractéristique d'une époque que d'un écrivain' (*2*, 654), Marivaux was one of a growing number of writers who projected love as an analogue of economic activity: the exchange of property spills over into the exchange of feelings. Marianne is 'un trésor' and her 'vraies richesses' are her affective qualities. Jacob's heart is 'plus précieux que tout l'or du monde': it is not 'une marchandise'. It was a view of love which appealed to readers who were losing patience not only with romance but with the idea of romance. But more particularly, it reflected the upper middle class values of the *salons* of Mme de Lambert and Mme de Tencin which Marivaux himself admired.

Though Marivaux was no social reformer, his values clearly challenged the status quo. Jacob and Marianne do not fit easily into society and their honesty and integrity prove to be a disruptive influence. Climal is discredited, Valville learns that it is not enough to play the attentive lover, M. Doucin is exposed, Mme de Ferval is embarrassed: none finds it possible to sustain a façade of respectability in their company. 'Quelle dangereuse petite fille tu es', remarks Mme de Miran (*4*, 196); 'tu es le plus dangereux petit bonhomme que je connaisse', confesses Mme de Ferval (*6*, 165). They belong to a new 'aristocracy of the heart' and they enshrine values which Marivaux readily associated with the charge-holding and investor class. In presenting them as 'smuggled goods' (*6*, 240), he clearly found no contradiction between their pure intentions and a hard-headed taste for results. And in much the same spirit, he was to succeed in steering the novel, still in essentials an aristocratic form of literature, towards bourgeois realism.

## 5 *Art and technique*

Marivaux's journals were launched as commercial speculations. Appearing irregularly in small parts, their survival depended on demand. The fate of his early novels was similarly determined by the reaction of his public. The first three parts of *Les Effets* were sufficiently popular to justify the publication not only of the rest but also of *La Voiture embourbée* and 'une autre plus considérable' (*1*, 311). In the event, *La Voiture embourbée* sold badly and *Pharsamon* never appeared. Even by 1730, when his reputation in the theatre should have made him a good risk for a publisher, he continued to follow the generalised practice (followed by Crébillon *fils*, Mouhy and many others) of testing the market before completing his manuscript.

The aesthetic implications of Marivaux's method of composition are considerable. The first part of *Marianne* was published in 1731 'pour voir ce qu'on en dira. Si elle plaît, le reste paraîtra successivement; il est tout prêt' (*4*, 47). Part 2 did not in fact appear for three years and, though the 'Avertissement' suggests that readers particularly liked the 'réflexions', Marivaux was in reality sensitive to the criticisms made by a number of reviewers (see *3*, lxvff.) of Marianne's 'babil'. In later parts, the narrative pace quickens and nowhere more so than in the history of Tervire, the three books of which were published together in 1742. And just as the tempo of the whole accelerates, so the rhythm of individual episodes reflects Marivaux's need to raise his readers' expectations: certain of Dickens's novels which first appeared as newspaper serials are similarly punctuated by dramatic crises originally designed to persuade the public to buy the next issue. Part 2 ends with a knock at the door. Has Favier talked (Part 5)? What does Valville's letter say (Part 7)? What answer will Marianne give the 'officier'? Will the nun's story be as exciting as promised (Part 8)?

It is quite clear that Marivaux no more knew the answers to these questions than his public. *Marianne* was not 'tout prêt' and its heroine's regular recapitulations of the story so far were designed to bring new readers up to date. Marivaux loses track of names – there are two Villots and Mme de Miran first appears as Mme de Valville – and Marianne 'forgets' to give us Père Vincent's reply to her letter (*4*, 230). He tries to plan ahead ('comme la suite va le prouver', 'vous le verrez dans la suite') but he does not always fulfil his promises. The portrait of Mme Dorsin promised in Part 4 spills over into Part 5; Tervire's story, announced in Part 4, does not materialise until Part 9 when it takes over so completely that D'Alembert was led to wonder whether Marivaux had not embarked on a new and separate novel. Of course, Marianne claims to have a 'plan' (*4*, 251) and Marivaux turns her lapses to good use by making them a part of that 'indolence' which characterises her older self. The human truth of her tale is enhanced by her honest amateurism, for she writes as she talks: 'les idées me gagnent, je suis femme, je conte mon histoire' (*4*, 91). This stratagem does not disguise that fact that *Marianne* is under-planned and carelessly reliant on coincidence – Mme de Miran conveniently turns out to be Valville's mother, for example – and on those narrative clichés which Marivaux plundered from other authors and from his own early novels, as Deloffre has shown (*3*, iiiff.): the coaching accident which features in *La Voiture embourbée* recurs in the attack which orphans Marianne and again in the conversion of Mme de Sainte-Hermières. There are misdirected letters, death-bed confessions and recognition scenes, while within the covers of *Marianne* a number of narrative parallels are visible: the nun preyed upon by her 'jeune Tartuffe' recalls Climal's designs on Marianne, while Mme de Sainte-Hermières's repentance echoes Climal's change of heart. The book could conceivably have ended with the marriage of Marianne, but Marivaux relaunches his story by making Valville's fickleness the source of new adventures. At such times, we may feel that we are reading a series of variations on familiar themes which could be continued indefinitely.

On the other hand, *Le Paysan* was published consecutively – between April 1734 and April 1735 – and not surprisingly shows fewer signs of carelessness (though Agathe first appeared as Javote) and Jacob's story is summarised less frequently. Similar promises are made but are better kept, perhaps because the proportion of reflections to adventures is here reversed. The practice of ending each episode with an anticipation of the next is less noticeable,

but it remains a feature of Marivaux's technique: Part 3 sends Jacob
to visit Mme de Ferval and Part 5 advertises theatre gossip to come.
Nor can we feel sure that Marivaux was working to a clearly defined
plan. He seems to be at the mercy of his imagination as he drops or
retains certain characters: Catherine is suppressed just as she is acquiring a personality, while Mme d'Orville, M. Doucin and Mme
d'Alain are not named until their functional usefulness to the plot is
well established. Coincidence remains a major means of articulating
plot: when a situation seems to be played out, Marivaux points it
arbitrarily in a new direction by killing off Jacob's master or by
enabling him to meet Mlle Habert or Dorsan.

If both novels suffer from the demands of serial publication, they
also reveal the limitations of Marivaux's inventiveness and technique.
His 'portraits' are undramatic and though there is more action in
*Le Paysan* than in *Marianne*, Marivaux regularly employs the 'tableau'
(the narrative equivalent of the 'portrait') to highlight a moment by
immobilising events: the deaths of Climal and Dursan, for example,
have their equivalent in shorter stoppages in which Jacob shows us
Mme de Ferval 'en négligé' (6, 161) or the effect of M. Doucin's
unexpected arrival at the wedding which turns all present into
'statues' who do not move for 'bien deux minutes' (6, 106). This
last scene is similar in structure and function to the equally coin-
cidental arrival of Mme Dutour at the house of Mme de Fare, and is
one of many narrative parallels which may be drawn between the
two novels: Jacob is summoned before a magistrate and Marianne
before a President and while the mood is different in each case, the
pattern is identical. Although the overall shape of both novels is
loose, the quest to 'parvenir' remains constant, as does the 'double
registre' which gives it psychological depth.

Marivaux's art as a novelist was clearly restricted both by the
requirements of commerce and by the conventions of fiction. Yet
he not only accepted the limitations imposed on him but reacted
with considerable imagination. His originality lay not in escaping
from the traditions of narrative but in his varied use of them and,
above all, in his concern for psychological rather than documentary
realism. *Marianne* and *Le Paysan* are fundamentally distinct in their
treatment of a common design. *Marianne* belongs in the line of
sentimental and analytical novels which runs from the *roman précieux*

of La Calprenède, Gomberville and Mlle de Scudéry through the exfoliations of passion and love of Mme de La Fayette into the eighteenth century's fascination with the human heart. *Le Paysan*, on the other hand, springs from an earthier vein of comic realism compounded of the low-life vulgarity of Scarron and the morally dubious but entertaining escapades of the Spanish *pícaro*. Marivaux's achievement as a novelist, in historical terms, was to have lowered the first and raised the second to a point where, though they do not meet, they indicate the road ahead towards a recognisably modern concept of psychological and material realism.

The common link between them is Marivaux's subtle sense of the comic. Though he sometimes suffers from bouts of indignation — Tervire's story, on the whole, is a sombre affair — he gravitated temperamentally towards 'le plaisant', an urbane sense of irony and amused tolerance. He had little taste for satire, which he considered cruel and unjust (*6*, 137), nor did he attempt the broader effects of farce save in a somewhat sparing use of ploys (Jacob eavesdropping, for instance) drawn from the theatrical tradition. He much preferred situations (Tervire and her poacher, Marianne and her ankle, Jacob and his clothes) which show the discrepancy between what we claim to be and what we are. To be sure, there are occasional jokes: Jacob's father turning round in puzzlement when addressed as 'monsieur' by his nephews; the description of the drunken valet as 'l'ennemi juré' of water (*6*, 49); or the repeated jests about the age of women. But most of the humour derives from the way in which Marivaux's narrators laugh at their younger selves. Marianne's youthful vanity is the source of much amused comment and Jacob's 'naïveté' is subjected to mild, good-natured criticism. Though they do not set up as moral judges, their wry presence is a constant reminder of Marivaux's humane values. If Marivaux was 'mon propre spectateur, comme le spectateur des autres' (*2*, 232), Marianne and Jacob similarly combine the roles of watcher and participant: they exist both inside and outside a play and that play is the human comedy. Marivaux's sense of humour — an essential ingredient of the intelligent heart — saved him from sentimentality and from heavy moralising. His world is informed by a comic vision which, if it denied him access to the deepest passions, isolates the delusions which govern our lives.

Nowhere are his perceptions sharper than in the area of language. His religious bigots are as skilled as Tartuffe in draping their base and selfish desires in the most pious sentiments — from M. de Climal to the Habert sisters and any number of narrow-minded *dévotes* pledged to spreading not Christian sweetness and light but the misery and spite which their misshapen sensiblities take pleasure in inflicting on others. The words they speak are opaque and their incongruity is exploited to its full comic potential. When Mme Rémy locks the door, Mme de Ferval protests that 'elle nous enferme' but in such a way that Jacob understands her to mean: 'Nous voilà donc seuls' (*6*, 204). In the ensuing conversation we too can see that, by defending weakly, Mme de Ferval is in fact encouraging strongly. Marivaux's use of language thus becomes a major means of distinguishing between surface appearances and that inner reality which is the lasting object of his presentation of character and which underpins his whole system of values. Words are shorn of the approximate meanings of accepted usage. Marianne in particular has a great love of precise definitions (not only of difficult concepts like 'vanité' but also of simpler terms like 'ancien' and 'vieux' (*4*, 272)) which warn us against oversimplifying reality by the use of general concepts which deny the particular and the unique. The very names we give to people not only distort their reality but also reveal our prejudices. The 'petite aventurière' who turned Valville's head was, says Mme de Miran, a 'grisette en ses beaux jours de fête' (*4*, 175-8): it is a description of herself which Marianne rejects as untrue. In the same way, the abbess, mistaking her for a wealthy recruit, calls her 'belle enfant' and 'mon ange'; but the moment she learns the truth, she says 'mademoiselle' and even 'ma pauvre enfant': 'ma pauvre!' exclaims Marianne, 'quelle différence de style! Auparavant elle m'avait dit: ma belle' (*4*, 162). Jacob too is keenly aware of the importance of names as signs and grows angry when inappropriate terms falsify truth: his nephews call his father 'Monsieur' as though to absorb his reality into their world and no greater insult can be proferred than the Chevalier's 'Mons Jacob' which is a denial of the social and human progress he has made as M. de la Vallée.

But Marivaux's use of language is more than either a comic ploy or even an analytical tool: it is at the heart of his portrayal of his world. The abstraction of his 'portraits' and 'réflexions' is relieved by lively images, expressions and proverbial sayings which certain readers found vulgar. However, Aubert de la Chenaie was one of many who reacted more positively. If Marivaux's diction 'n'est pas naturelle, elle est ingénieuse et les sujets qu'il traite, quelques indifférents qu'ils soient, deviennent intéressants entre ses mains'.[5] Marivaux was accustomed to adverse criticism of his neologisms and 'unnatural' linguistics tendencies, yet he persisted not only in allowing his characters to speak in accordance with their social status but also with their character. Mme Dutour's speech reflects both her background and her personality: 'ses expressions allaient comme son esprit, qui allait comme il plaisait à son peu de malice et de finesse' (*4*, 77). Mme d'Alain's 'bonté de cœur babillarde' tells us as much about her as it does about her origins (*6*, 83). The coachman, Mme Rémy and Catherine identify themselves socially and individually by the way they speak, for each has a personal style, just as the jailer has 'un style de geôlier' (*6*, 142) or Agathe's malice is expressed by the 'style' of her sort (*6*, 116). The clearest instance, of course, is provided by Jacob himself, for his social and moral progress is charted scrupulously in linguistic terms. 'On distingue aisément le discours de la Campagne et celui de la Ville', continues Aubert (pp. 31-2): 'on s'aperçoit du changement qu'opèrent dans un Villageois l'usage et la fréquentation de personnes d'une éducation plus cultivée. Les degrés en sont si marqués, qu'il n'a pas besoin d'avertir le lecteur'. Jacob is conscious of his departures from accepted norms and frequently excuses an image or an effusion with a 'pour ainsi dire' or a 'comme on dirait'. Yet like the Marivaux of the essay *Sur la clarté du discours* or the sixth number of *Le Cabinet du Philosophe* (*2*, 52-6, 380-7), he believes that the human soul feels far more things than it has words for and claimed for it 'la liberté de se servir des expressions du mieux qu'elle pourrait, pourvu qu'on entendît clairement ce qu'elle voudrait dire, et qu'elle ne pût employer d'autres termes sans diminuer ou altérer sa pensée' (*6*, 237). Thus if he describes himself as a 'figure de contrabande', he apologises but explains that there is nothing 'qui signifie mieux ce que je veux dire que cette expression qui n'est pas trop noble' (*6*, 240). It is in this context that we must understand his remark that 'chacun a sa façon de s'exprimer, qui vient de sa façon de sentir'

---

[5] *Lettres amusantes et critiques sur les romans*, Amsterdam, 1743, pp. 30-1.

(*6*, 26). It is a dictum which applies to all of Marivaux's characters. Marianne wonders 'où voulez-vous que je prenne un style?... je ne sais pas seulement ce que c'est. Comment fait-on pour avoir un?' (*4*, 50-1). She does not believe it can be learnt from the study of good authors; it emerges naturally from the unaffected recording of what she thinks and feels. Jacob's style is racy and popular, peppered with lively images and sayings. Marianne's is characterised by a more refined search for subtle analysis, a taste for maxims and a liking for unexpected changes of tense which heighten the drama. If men and women are 'porteurs de visages' which are distinctive and transparent (*2*, 124), their 'façon de parler' is no less revealing.

'Le marivaudage' thus emerges not only as a marvellously supple and exact tool of psychological analysis but as the corner stone of Marivaux's realism. Not only are his characters allowed to portray themselves through what they say and how they speak, they are no less clearly exhibited in his narrators' tone of voice. Marianne neatly renders her suitor's 'pesantes et grossières protestations de tendresse' (*4*, 281-5), while the overpowering Mme de Fécour springs to life as Jacob describes one of her exits: 'Et là-dessus, elle embrasse Mme de Ferval qui la remercie, qu'elle remercie, s'appuie sans façon sur mon bras, m'emmène, me fait monter dans son carrosse, m'y appelle tantôt monsieur, tantôt mon bel enfant, m'y parle comme si nous nous fussions connus depuis dix ans, toujours cette grosse gorge en avant, et nous arrivons chez elle' (*6*, 172). It is a breathless, tumbling description which itself extends our knowledge of her in the most graphic way. If each character has his personal 'façon de s'exprimer', Marivaux's sensitively orchestrated narrative style is a no less subtle means of expressing a total personality within the framework of his values.

Yet however vivid this glimpse of Mme de Fécour might be, it also reveals Marivaux's impatience with more conventional notations of reality, and in particular with the specifics of time and place. Though the general chronology of both novels is carefully recorded ('le lendemain', 'le surlendemain', etc.), time expands alarmingly to accommodate events. For instance, the day Jacob travels to Versailles, meets Mme D'Orville, returns to Paris, visits Mme de Fécour and breaks with Mme de Ferval, lasts as long as Marivaux wants it to. Moreover, though the 'Avertissement' situates Marianne's arrival in

Paris in about 1665, a subsequent reference to the Jacobite troubles
(*4*, 314-5) would seem to place events somewhere around 1690—
even though the mood seems nearer to the 1720s where Valville,
that 'contemporain des amants de notre temps' (*4*, 336), appears to
belong. Some readers may even have recognised Fleury in the
President or Mme de Lambert in Mme de Miran, or taken the comment that Tervire is 'un exemple du triomphe de la grâce' (*4*, 399) as
an echo of the Jansenist troubles of the 1730s. A similar confusion is
noticeable in the adventures of Jacob, who presumably was young
around the turn of the century. He occasionally reminds us of the
passage of time from the 'then' of events to 'ce temps où j'écris'
(*6*, 211), but his adventures too seem less historical than modern.
Such uncertainties in the handling of the time of the narration and
of the time of the action occasionally pose difficulties and may
interfere with the 'double registre' to the point where we wonder
which Marianne or which Jacob is speaking. Yet overall the pattern
is clear enough and Marivaux's lapses do not vitiate his technique.
Indeed scenes like those in which Marianne's reactions overlay Mme
de Miran's worries about the 'grisette', or where Jacob filters the
overheard conversation between Mme de Ferval and the Chevalier,
have all the harmonics of advanced narrative counterpoint. There
are, of course, awkward moments: the sudden arrival of Valville
and his mother at the President's house is explained by a long
account of their enquiries into Marianne's whereabouts within a
time scale which fits only if we accept an absent 'tourière' and
Mme de Miran's slight indisposition (*4*, 293). In much the same
way, Marianne must justify her total recall of Tervire's long tale
and does it brazenly by saying: 'je me ressouviens de ce que la
religieuse m'a dit, de même que je me ressouviens de ce qui m'est
arrivé' (*4*, 469). Technical difficulties with first-person narratives
are not uncommon in eighteenth-century novels and in the main
Marivaux handles them well. Yet by lighting the foreground so
brilliantly, he dims the background and his narrow focus, though
it illuminates the inner reality of his characters, fixes our attention
on the immediate present of a two-dimensional world.

He is no more eager to locate events in space than in time. Scenes
change with a perfunctory 'nous voici arrivés' or a 'dispensez-moi
de ces détails' as we are hurried from one stage of the plot to the

next. There are no descriptions of Paris, of Marianne's village or of Mme Dursan's country-house. We see little of the prison in which Jacob is detained nor are we told exactly where Marianne's coach was attacked. Mlle Habert's home is accurately situated in the rue des Monnaies, but her interior is presented in abstract terms: 'Netteté, simplicité, et propreté, c'est ce qu'on y voyait' (6, 57). If Jacob's suit and Marianne's 'hardes' are described in some detail, it is because they tell us something about their mood and character and not because such information is intrinsically interesting. We do not learn how to rent an appartment, how nuns take their vows or how to find an official at Versailles: Jacob notes simply that 'il me fallut traverser plusieurs cours . . . et enfin on m'introduisit dans un grand cabinet' (6, 187). Yet just as Marivaux's presentation of character progresses from abstract 'portraits' to individualised sketches, so he moves from the vague setting of the classical novel to more precise indications of the life which goes on behind the action occupying the front of his stage. We see how a bourgeois heir becomes an 'anobli' (6, 26), how the country nobility arrange their marriages (4, 381-9), how debtors are evicted (4, 483-6) and, very memorably, how coachmen behave. If Marivaux omits to describe places and interiors which were only too familiar to his readers, he went out of his way to show areas of Parisian society which they did not know. He gives Mme Dutour her head and draws some illuminating class distinctions: the coachman calls her a 'chiffon-nière' whereas she thinks of herself as a 'bourgeoise' (4, 115). Tervire differentiates clearly between the conduct of 'demoiselles' and 'bourgeoises' (4, 397-8) and there is enough concrete detail for us to situate Jacob's family in the 'cultivateur' class. Jacob's story, which is set on a lower social level, is particularly revealing of ordi-nary life. He lets us see and hear the populace, and categorises Mme d'Alain very precisely. Catherine's speech, even if it is shorn of the 'Dieu soit béni' which normally punctuates it, is accurately observed and carefully rendered. Jacob occasionally becomes a journalist of the 'fait divers' who provides brief glimpses into the lives of people who have no importance to the plot: the circum-stances of the murder (6, 148), of the traveller's marriage (6, 177-184), D'Orville's past and Dorsan's story (6, 233-7). Money, banished as ignoble by the genteel novel, figures prominently in both stories: Brunon acquires a fortune and Mme Dutour haggles over a few *sous*. Food, a no less vulgar subject, makes regular appearances: the Habert's larder contains fresh eggs, jam, 'un reste de ragoût', cold fowl, wine and 'le bon pain' which is one of Jacob's highly prized early successes. Marivaux, for all his documentary reticence, here creates an atmosphere of tangible reality which he intended as a revolutionary innovation. Readers who were scandalised that a coachman's ill-temper and the life of a 'lingère' should be thought fit subjects for a novel, he says, are simply victims of the worst kind of social snobbery. The 'cœur humain' is interesting wherever it beats, and unprejudiced readers 'ne seront pas fâchés de voir ce que c'est que l'homme dans un cocher, et ce que c'est que la femme dans une petite marchande'. To identify noble hearts with 'les grandes conditions' is to ignore the rest of humanity and to argue that being bourgeois is an affront to nature (*4*, 86, 87). Behind Marivaux's selective documentary realism lies the desire to widen the scope of literature itself.

For while he does not fail to state that his novels are intended to please and instruct, his claim that they are truth not fiction goes considerably further than the usual tactic of the novelist who sought to defend the genre and make his work respectable. 'Ce n'est point ici une histoire forgée à plaisir' (*6*, 26), says Jacob, and Marianne's memoirs, though authenticated by an 'editor', not only run counter to the popular demand for adventures, but are presented less as a carefully composed book, a 'livre à imprimer' (*4*, 50), than as a spontaneous recollection. Both *Marianne* and *Le Paysan* consistently use the word 'roman' to signify events and reactions which are exaggerated and false: indeed, when Marianne adopts a 'ton romanesque' in recounting her life to Varthon, the effect is not what she anticipated (*4*, 320). Marivaux himself intervenes to berate the reader who is offended by Valville's fickleness. A 'héros de roman', he says, would not perhaps be so crass but such things happen in real life: Marianne's story reflects 'l'instabilité des choses humaines, et non pas des aventures d'imagination qui vont comme on veut' (*4*, 335). It is an argument which Marivaux also puts up against Crébillon *fils* who stands accused of resorting to the imagination which favours the 'romanesque' above 'le vrai' (*6*, 185-7).

Marivaux's performance, technically, is in many ways crude and defective. Not only is he careless with details, but he resorts to narrative clichés, happily suppresses characters who have served their purpose and over-uses coincidence. He also has a marked habit of arranging arbitrary changes of heart as a means of moving his story in a new direction: Climal repents, Brunon turns nasty and Valville betrays Marianne. Yet in spite of his faults, both *Marianne* and *Le Paysan* have the impact of reality which Marivaux clearly worked for. There are moments which have the immediacy of theatre − the 'scène muette' between Jacob and his mistress, or the conversation with Mme de Ferval which reveals his unease as he sharpens her pen − and the 'double registre' generates a remarkable depth of dramatic counterpoint which at times anticipates Stendhal. Though we know that Marianne and Jacob are artful 'authors', Marivaux sustains the illusion of artless self-portrayal which, though it falters on the narrative level, stems from a total concern for psychological realism. He possessed his characters completely and his closeness to them results in the brilliantly lit projection of that internal reality which was not only the focal point of his sincerely felt values but the object of his marvellously exact and supple prose style.

Since Marivaux understood Jacob and Marianne so perfectly, we may wonder why he never completed their adventures − even though he was asked to do so many times during the twenty years he lived after the publication of the last parts of *Marianne*. The level of demand was high if we judge not only by the number of imitations that appeared but also by the various attempts that were made to finish his novels for him. A conclusion to *Marianne* appeared prematurely in 1739 and a final Book Twelve was added anonymously in 1745 some two years after Mrs Collyer had provided her own ending for her English translation, *The Virtuous Orphan*, while Mme Riccoboni's elegant and sympathetic 'suite' appeared during the winter of 1760-1. *Le Paysan* was completed in three supplementary parts in 1756. These continuations, with varying degrees of success, take note of Marivaux's own vague plans for finishing his stories. D'Orville and Mlle Habert were to die and Jacob was to make his fortune through Dorsan and find love with Mme D'Orville; Marianne, after digesting the lessons Tervire draws from her experiences, will decide against the convent life, will once more be loved by Valville 'sous une figure qu'il ne connaît pas encore' (*4*, 336) before becoming the Comtesse de *** of the title. But if Marivaux had a general idea of the direction his novels were to take, the fact remains that he leaves Marianne listening forever to Tervire and Jacob locked in conversation at the Comédie Française.

It has been suggested that Marivaux the novelist, like Marivaux the journalist who frequently broke off in mid-anecdote when his journal died under him, ran into publishing difficulties of some sort. It could be, for instance, that he was one victim of the 'proscription des romans' which Georges May has uncovered (*13*, 75-105). As a result of mounting moral pressures, the Chancelier Daguesseau, in 1737, began refusing permission to print to all save the most wholesome novels. As a result, most novelists were driven to publish abroad, novels became accordingly more expensive and therefore harder to sell. It is unlikely that *Le Paysan* would have passed the 'wholesome' test nor, so it would seem, did *Marianne*: Part 7 was published in Paris in February 1737, just before the ban became effective, but Part 8, which appeared later that year, was printed at The Hague. Marivaux may well have intended to continue both novels, but having run foul of Daguesseau's censorship and of its commercial consequences, saw his characters go cold on him. Certainly, the three parts of *Marianne* which came out in 1742 seem to relegate Marianne to a minor role and it is Tervire – a noticeably more virtuous and indeed wholesome young lady – who seems to have his attention.

Be this as it may, most critics of Marivaux prefer to adduce aesthetic reasons for his failure to complete his novels. Deloffre, for instance, suggests that first-person narratives are by definition unfinishable: 'le personnage qui raconte sa vie peut-il conclure?' (*3*, xlix). E.J.H. Greene argues that Marivaux had, in *Marianne*, 'painted himself into a corner' from which there was no satisfactory exit (*11*, 184-5). And if Marivaux the playwright was obliged to bring proceedings to a conclusion by the very nature of theatre, his inability to end his novels, it is suggested, stemmed from that 'paresse' of which he occasionally speaks.

Yet it may simply be that Marivaux had no more to say. The five parts of *Le Paysan parvenu* and the first eight of *Marianne* follows the personal evolution of his principal characters to the point where they are virtually in full possession of themselves:

Marianne is acquiring control of her destiny and Jacob is close to becoming a gentleman. Their further adventures would be little more than adventures for, apart from the narrative formalities, they are on the edge of knowing who they are. When Marivaux did return to Marianne, he gives every impression of having lost interest in her in favour of a new sensibility – that of Tervire – which he proceeds to direct and shape until the moment when she too begins to exhibit that 'fierté de sentiment' which is a kind of graduation certificate. Marivaux's plays depict the dawning of love; his novels show the dawning of identity. There is every reason therefore to think that Marivaux, always far more interested in people than in plots, in psychological realism rather than in narrative problems, in middles rather than beginnings or ends, halted his stories because they were already as complete as he wished to make them.

## 6 *Conclusion*

Marivaux was a private man who lived in an age which preferred public attitudes. Van Loo's portrait – typically, it is the only portrait we have of him – shows a round-faced, middle-aged man surprised in mid-gesture, beaming uncertainly, his eyes not quite meeting those of the observer. He spoke little of himself nor is he visible in what he wrote, even at the deepest level. If we set Racine's obsession with dominant females against his motherless youth, we may perceive something of his unconscious drives. But such a test is valueless when applied to Marivaux. His novels may feature few fathers and many kindly maternal women, but before we jump to hasty conclusions about his 'feminine' sensibility, we should remember that in his plays kindness and affection are shown by more fathers than mothers. His life, like his personality, remains mysterious and his biography – in spite of strenuous efforts made in the last thirty years to give him a face – amounts to little more than an account of his literary career. His contemporaries saw several different men in him: the bore who ruined the flow of *salon* conversation while he ransacked his vocabulary for the *mot juste*, the charitable soul who gave his money to the needy, the fluent conversationalist eternally at pains to draw out the best in others and the tightwad who borrowed from his housekeeper.

His personal standing was never high and he projected no very definite image to his public. He gives every appearance of knowing himself very well without being either particularly impressed or disappointed by his conclusions. Indeed, it would seem that Marivaux, a far better psychologist than a novelist, was too well-adjusted to feel those deep urges out of which great literature is made. His characters face no implacable destiny and the love that comes unexpectedly is never a tearing, raging passion but a bundle of feelings to be ordered and savoured. His world is a world of reasonableness and accommodations. For if he was a man of feeling, he also had a great deal of common sense which told him that literature is one thing and life quite another: it is a demonstrable fact that more people survive love than die of it. If Marivaux found it difficult to take great passion seriously, it was because he was too sane, too passionless and too civilised.

Extreme only in his moderation, was Marivaux no more than a decadent writer who produced a kind of mellow coda to the great symphonic poems of the seventeenth century? After the short-lived successes of the 1720s and 1730s, his century quickly wearied of him. His novels continued to be read and certain of his plays remained in the repertoire, but the new, more militant mood was against him. His subtle, non-doctrinaire dissections of the human heart seemed a luxury to a generation which set out to free humanity from shackles which had never inconvenienced the author of *Marianne* and *Le Paysan* – the oppressions, superstitions and injustices which Voltaire called 'l'infâme'. He was attacked for his modernist stance, which was held accountable for both his 'style précieux et affecté' and his tedious concern with the lesser intricacies of human experience (his 'métaphysique alambiquée de l'amour'). He was too controlled to satisfy pre-romantic sensibilities and he was too 'sensible' for the rationalists. Both in the cast of his mind and in the conduct of his literary affairs, there was a degree of contrariness which could not but set him at odds with the intellectual establishment. As a young man, he did not arm himself with the five-act verse tragedy which was the only road to literary fortune, but began with a novel, a form of writing which was regarded as suspect. Quickly wearying of the heroic romance which had fired his imagination, he fell to ridiculing the genre with comic epics of a kind that was considered not only unfashionable but vulgar. Thence he moved to journalism, which had yet to be accepted as a calling, before turning to the theatre. Here again it was not tragedy that drew him (*Annibal* (1720) was a failure which he never repeated) but comedy, another second-class literary mode. He preferred prose to verse, one act to five and the Théâtre Italien to the prestigious Théâtre Français which alone could confer a measure of honour on the comic author. Moreover, he avoided the comedy of character and manners bequeathed by Molière and chose instead to explore more insubstantial states of mind – those 'marivaudages' which Voltaire described as so many butterfly eggs in a spider's web. It is possible that Marivaux simply recognised his limitations. But it is more likely that he deliberately exploited his strengths.

Though he had ideas — he shows how 'l'esprit' may be turned by 'le cœur' into a source of moral integrity — he had no intellectual curiosity to speak of. As a Christian, he failed to see the interest of the clockmaker God. As a moralist, he was more concerned with human nature as it is than with the general principles by which men should live. Though he knew Fontenelle who did so much to popularise science, he gives no indication that he had ever heard of Newton, the immediate begetter of his century's scientific optimism. His concern was with feelings rather than with right reason and his interest was descriptive rather than prescriptive (as it was to be with Rousseau): a matter for report and not a source of abstract ideas. By temperament more than by conviction, Marivaux was an *anti-philosophe.*

The English novelists regarded him highly as a copyer of nature, as a satirist of manners and as a novelist who, by rescuing the genre from the excesses both of farce and of romance, had steered it towards that picture of man in society which was the proper province of the novel (see 7, xiii-xvi). In France, though he was after Voltaire the most performed living playwright, his narrow range, 'precious' style, his preoccupation with low-key emotions and his reluctance to commit himself to the literature of ideas, all relegated him to the second, even the third division of writers. Moreover, he had the misfortune to lose most of his creative impulse twenty years before his death and lived to see his work fall into neglect. 'Fontenelle a engendré Marivaux', noted Piron cruelly, 'Marivaux a engendré Moncrif, et Moncrif n'engendra rien.'

Regarded neither as a major literary figure nor ever dismissed as a minor author, Marivaux remained a name to conjure with. *Marianne* and *Le Paysan parvenu* were re-published and though they never acquired disciples, the persistent taste for a certain kind of preciosity continued to be associated with them. Dorat and Florian took to him but La Harpe accused him of myopia. It is true that Marivaux preferred the microscope to the telescope in his explorations of human nature, but it was his short focus and not La Harpe's long sight which was to prevail. Without ever being a popular author, Marivaux has shown a sturdy capacity for surviving changes in taste.

His work possesses qualities of permanent value, for in an age which set sectarian limits upon that freedom to think which it proclaimed to be one of its greatest aims, Marivaux went his own way. The very concept of 'marivaudage' which his contemporaries turned against him, was in a real sense revolutionary in nature. By refusing to share the fashion for militant opinions and by rejecting the current aesthetic ideals, he staked his claim for the independence of the artist to present the world in his own terms. He followed his natural inclinations and did not allow himself to be bound by taste. He chose to write about people as he saw them and he remained true to his own method of expression. If his critics regarded him as an eccentric, it was because his art was premature. He was an individual in a century which admired conformity to accepted standards of behaviour and attitudes. When we read him, we stand to learn a great deal from his acute observation of human conduct and motive, for he is an experimental psychologist rather than the doctrinaire proposer of a theoretical view of human nature. That we can still respond to the freshness of his analyses must be attributed to the fact that Marivaux was an early champion of the right of the artist, generally acknowledged only since the time of the Romantics, to show his world in his own way.

# Bibliography

## WORKS BY MARIVAUX

1. *Œuvres de jeunesse*, ed. Frédéric Deloffre, Gallimard, Bibliothèque de la Pléiade, 1972.

2. *Journaux et œuvres diverses*, ed. F. Deloffre and Michel Gilot, Garnier, 1969.

3. *La Vie de Marianne*, ed. F. Deloffre, Garnier, 1963 (first published in 1957).

4. *La Vie de Marianne*, ed. M. Gilot, Garnier-Flammarion, 1978.

5. *Le Paysan parvenu*, ed. F. Deloffre, Garnier, 1965 (first published in 1959).

6. *Le Paysan parvenu*, ed. M. Gilot, Garnier-Flammarion, 1965.

7. *The Virtuous Orphan or, The Life of Marianne Countess of \*\*\**, [translated] *by Mrs Mary Mitchell Collyer*, ed. W.H. McBurney and M.F. Shugrue, Southern Illinois Press, 1965.

## STUDIES

8. Henri Coulet, *Marivaux romancier*, Corti, 1974.

9. Henri Coulet and Michel Gilot, *Marivaux, un humanisme expérimental*, Larousse, 1973.

10. Frédéric Deloffre, *Une Préciosité nouvelle: Marivaux et le marivaudage* (second ed.), A. Colin, 1967.

11. E.J.H. Greene, *Marivaux*, University of Toronto Press, 1965.

12. Ruth K. Jamieson, *Marivaux, a Study in Sensibility*, New York, 1941 (reissued by Octagon Books, 1969).

13. Georges May, *Le Dilemme du roman au XVIIIe siècle (1715-1761)*, Presses Universitaires de France, 1963.

14. Vivienne Mylne, *The Eighteenth Century French Novel. Technique of Illusion*, Manchester University Press, 1965 (pp. 104-124); revised edition, Cambridge University Press, 1981 (pp. 104-24).

15. Georges Poulet, *Etudes sur le temps humains*, Plon, 1952 (vol. II, pp. 1-34).

16. Ronald C. Rosbottom, *Marivaux's Novels. Theme and Function in Early Eighteenth Century Narrative*, Fairleigh Dickinson University Press and London, Associated University Presses, 1974.

17. Jean Rousset, 'Marivaux et la structure du double registre', *Studi Francesi*, 1957, pp. 58-68; reprinted in the author's *Forme et signification*, Corti, 1962, pp. 45-64.

18. Leo Spitzer, 'A propos de *La Vie de Marianne*, lettre à M. Georges Poulet', in *Romanic Review*, 1953, pp. 102-106 (a reply to no. *15*).